Hiking

Wyoming's Teton and Washakie Wilderness Areas

Lee Mercer and Ralph Maughan

Published in cooperation with
The Wilderness Society

FALCON®

HELENA, MONTANA

A FALCON GUIDE®

Falcon® Publishing is continually expanding its list of recreational guidebooks. All books include detailed descriptions, accurate maps, and all information necessary for enjoyable trips. You can order extra copies of this book and get information and prices for other Falcon® books by writing Falcon, P.O. Box 1718, Helena, MT 59624, or by calling toll-free 1-800-582-2665. Also, please ask for a copy of our current catalog. Visit our website at www.Falcon.com or contact us by e-mail at falcon@falconguide.com.

All black-and-white photos by the authors unless otherwise noted.

Cataloging-in-Publication Data is on file at the Library of Congress.

Cover photo by Jeff Benjamin.

Project editor: Jay Nichols
Copy editor: Ann Seifert
Maps by Trapper Badovinac
Page compositor: Lynne Johnston
Book design by Falcon Publishing, Inc.

CAUTION
Outdoor recreational activities are by their very nature potentially hazardous. All participants in such activities must assume responsibility for their own actions and safety. The information contained in this guidebook cannot replace sound judgment and good decision-making skills, which help reduce exposure, nor does the scope of this book allow for the disclosure of all the potential hazards and risks involved in such activities.

Learn as much as possible about the outdoor recreational activities in which you participate, prepare for the unexpected, and be cautious. The reward will be a safer and more enjoyable experience.

 Text pages printed on recycled paper.

Contents

Absaroka Range

Front Range

The love of wilderness is more than a hunger for what is always beyond reach; it is also an expression of loyalty to the earth (the earth which bore us and sustains us); the only home we shall ever know, the only paradise we ever need, if only we had the eyes to see.

—Edward Abbey

*This book is in loving memory of Emily O. Hays (1972–1998).
I hope you took some of the medicine you found in this country
with you to the other side. Goodbye.*
Lee Mercer

Acknowledgments

The Teton and Washakie Wilderness Areas are an immense and little-known place. Hikers and backpackers are relatively new to the scene. A guidebook to such an area is a work in progress. It is a labor of love, first and foremost. So many people helped us along our journey that it is impossible to thank them all. Some, however, it is impossible not to.

Lee Mercer thanks Bob Beal, his hiking partner of 15 years. Without Bob's participation and enthusiasm, this book would simply not have been written. The route selections here reflect a burning passion for remote wilderness that evolved over many years between two people.

Lee also thanks Ralph and Jackie Maughan, whose counsel, friendship, and empathy have been invaluable over the last several years.

A number of people deserve special thanks for their contributions to this book. Thomas Bills and Connie Mock of the USDA Forest Service always answered all of our questions enthusiastically. Dennis Malburg of Jackson, Wyoming, provided shelter, friendship, and expert advice on auto mechanics. B. D. Weurfritz of Meeteetse, Wyoming, provided shelter, a nice book collection, and help with shuttles. Gwen Gerber provided us with Hike 7. Finally, Burns Briggs, the last of the old-time wilderness rangers, brought the prose of Norman MacLean to life before our very eyes. Thanks for all the stories and kindness, and for introducing us to the "red-faced bears."

A very special thanks to Anna Moscicki of Two Ocean Books in Dubois, Wyoming, for her advice and kindness.

Lee thanks the friendly folks of Park County, Wyoming, who always seem to have a good word and who never drive by a person without offering help, a cold drink, and hospitality."

Lee thanks all those who joined him for hikes. Their camaraderie was invaluable.

Overview Map

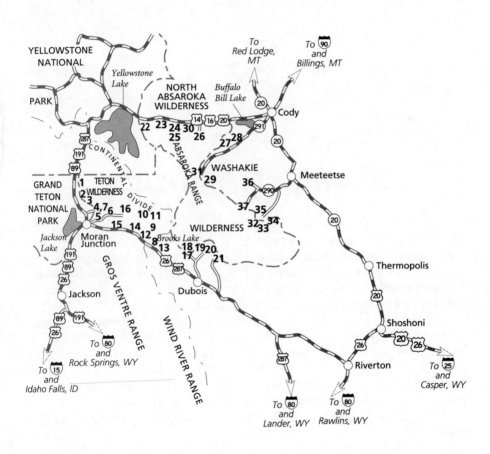

Legend

Interstate	(00)
US Highway	(00)
State or Other Principal Road	(00) (000)
Forest Road	435
Paved Road	⟹
Improved Road	⟹
Unimproved Road	========⟹
Trailhead	◯
Main Trail(s)/Route(s)	- - - - ⌒ - - -
Alternate/Secondary Trail(s)/Route(s)	- - - · ⌒ - · -
River/Creek	⌒⌒⌒
Meadows	米米米

Bridge	⌣ ⌢
Mountain Pass	) (
City	◯
Campground	▲
Cabins/Buildings	■
Peak/Elevation	9,782 ft.
Overlook/Point of Interest	◪
National Forest/Park Boundary	⌐ ⌐
Continental Divide	— · — · —
Map Orientation	N
Scale	0 0.5 1 Miles

Introduction

Traveling back and forth through Yellowstone's south entrance, millions of people glimpse the Teton's ramparts each year. Yet the country to the east is a curiosity, heightened by the sense of the Continental Divide stretching out there somewhere.

Yes, it is there, tracing the lonely heart of the wildest country in the lower 48. Just beyond the highway's roar, modern America fades and a primeval wilderness unfolds. This vast and magnificent landscape stretches east to the Bighorn Basin near Cody, Wyoming, and encompasses the headwaters of six major rivers. Above these rivers are vast tracts of subalpine and alpine country, where some of the most spectacular scenes in the contiguous 48 states can be witnessed—all in an awesome wilderness setting.

This is a book for those longing for spectacular scenery on a large scale and rugged landscape teeming with wildlife. This is a book for those who have tired of the crowds in the Wind River Range and in Glacier National Park and are longing for adventure in a true wilderness landscape.

THE TETON–WASHAKIE–SOUTHEAST YELLOWSTONE WILDERNESS COMPLEX

The Teton and Washakie Wilderness Areas are not, despite their immensity, isolated features. Together with southeast Yellowstone and some adjacent unprotected roadless areas, these lands make up one of the largest wilderness complexes in the continental United States. This seldom-seen area is vast in scale—more than 2 million acres. The Frank Church–River of No Return Wilderness in central Idaho is the only larger tract of unbroken wilderness in the United States south of Alaska. These lands are our last living reminder of what once was. This country remains much the same as when mountain man (and former member of the Lewis and Clark expedition) John Colter made his first exploration. Standing on a ridge, he became the first European-American to gaze at the Tetons.

THE FOUR PARTS

Mentally you can grasp the Teton and Washakie Wilderness Areas by thinking of them as made up of four parts. These parts, from west to east, are the Pinyon Peak Highlands, the Continental Divide, the Absaroka Range, and the Front Range—with the first two in the Teton Wilderness and the last two in the Washakie Wilderness.

The Pinyon Peak Highlands are subtle. Soft sedimentary rocks, formed in ancient seas, underlie this area. It is a land of ridges, valleys, and flower-filled meadows. Here you'll find many shallow ponds, wetlands, a few substantial lakes, and many creeks that tumble from their sources on high ridges. On top of the ridges, you'll find smooth river rocks, a reminder of this country's far-different geologic past.

1

Wildlife abounds in the Teton and Washakie Wilderness Areas. Bull elk on the Absaroka Trail.
LEE MERCER PHOTO

Much of the Pinyon Peak Highlands was burned in the Huck Fire of 1988, which was ignited on Labor Day weekend by a downed electrical wire near Flagg Ranch. It burned hot and fast. The loops in this guide try to maximize the green part of the mosaic created by the fire, but you will still walk through much burned forest.

The 1990s were wet, and many landslides in the Pinyon Peak Highlands, locally referred to as "blowouts," resulted from this moisture. They have affected many of the hikes. This activity is an ongoing seismological process and will continue for many years.

The Pinyon Peak Highlands see little or no use, except during hunting season, and is the wildest area described in this guide. Many of the trails are in poor condition. Although the topography is gentle, the poor trails, land-slides, and burned timber often make hiking slow. If your priority is isola-tion and you derive pleasure from challenges to your patience and will, this is the place for you.

The Continental Divide is a land of high volcanic mountains, massive plateaus, and big rivers. The Yellowstone, Snake, and Buffalo Rivers all begin here. Great walls of rotten breccia rock and broad, glacier-carved canyons intersperse with many beautiful meadows. The plateau tops are huge expanses of tundra with a few lakes and many ponds. The scenery from these plateaus is unmatched. The northern section of the Continental Divide burned extensively in the massive Mink Creek Fire of 1988. The Continental

Divide area is the busiest of the four parts, and many of the trails see considerable horse traffic. Of course, many routes see little or no traffic at all, and the scale of the country affords considerable privacy.

The Absaroka Range is a land dominated by rugged volcanic mountains and high plateaus that are dissected by deep drainages. The broken and eroded volcanic rocks have formed high-elevation buttes, mesas, and pinnacles. This is in stunning contrast to the deep and hidden forests found in the drainages. Sometimes you'll look up a stream and see a moose delicately crossing a creek. The immediate backdrop is a Douglas-fir–Engelmann spruce forest. In the distance, towering over everything, is a massive pinnacle with intricate columnar jointing patterns and a touch of snow on its summit.

During snowmelt, multitudes of waterfalls drop from the plateau tops to the forests and meadows below. Many of the drainages are linked by lofty passes, making this an outstanding destination for the backpacker seeking loop hikes with spectacular scenery, diverse habitat, and solitude.

The Front Range is a land of big peaks, high altitude, sparse tree cover, dry air, and relentless sun, relieved by occasional but often violent thunderstorms. Much of the Front Range lies outside the Washakie Wilderness and is open to "multiple use." Its future remains uncertain. It is drained by the spectacular and remote Wood and Greybull Rivers. Here, you'll see pronghorns browsing at 11,000 feet against a backdrop of Alaskan-scale scenery. The contrast of habitat types is beyond description—high desert biota exists in proximity to subalpine and even alpine habitats. Large expanses of

Wading a snowmelt-swollen tributary of Wolverine Creek on the west flank of Big Game Ridge, Teton Wilderness. RALPH MAUGHAN PHOTO

3

whitebark pine dominate the north slopes, while aspen, cottonwood, and Pacific willow appear in the riparian zones. Every turn in the trail reveals yet another magnificent scene with seemingly no end of big mountains. In short, this is a wilderness paradise.

The Teton and Washakie Wilderness Areas are the second-best place to see wildlife in Wyoming, behind only Yellowstone National Park. Moose, elk, and deer are very common. Bighorn sheep roam the high plateaus and ply the craggy summits of the Absaroka Range. Many nights, you can hear the mournful howl of coyotes. Mountain lion are present, and recent reports indicate that wolverine are returning to the area.

Since the wolf reintroduction in Yellowstone in 1995, wolf packs have formed in and near the wilderness areas, particularly the Teton Wilderness. The indigenous elk herds provide vast prey bases for the large and healthy wolves.

The Teton and Washakie Wilderness Areas are home to a large portion of the grizzly bear population in the Greater Yellowstone ecosystem. Most observers believe the grizzly population has increased in recent years, and there has clearly been a drift of grizzly bears southward and southeastward. The great bear can potentially be found anywhere in, or even near, the Teton and Washakie Wilderness Areas. You should assume there is at least one in every drainage (see "Be Bear Aware").

WEATHER

You should always be prepared for rain in the Teton and Washakie Wilderness Areas. It gets wetter as you head west, and the Tetons make their own weather. It can be pouring at Arizona Creek and sunny on Two Ocean Plateau, or vice versa. As you head east toward the Absaroka Range and the Front Range, it becomes drier and the intense sun dominates the weather. Here, an adequate supply of sunscreen is as important as good rain gear.

Some summers it will not rain for three weeks. Other times it will rain off and on every day for several weeks, especially in August. Some summers, monsoonal flows from the southwest affect the weather in the Teton and Washakie Wilderness Areas. During these periods it can rain very hard every day for two weeks. These patterns bring flash floods, destructive microbursts, landslides, and powerful lightning strikes.

At higher altitudes, the weather is often severe. Golf ball–sized hail, high winds, and frigid conditions predominate when it's just drizzling below. Above 10,000 feet, it snows at least a little bit every month of the year. Summer snows melt quickly, however.

The following is a general synopsis of weather conditions month by month:

June
June is usually a wet month. Rains of several days are common. Even in dry years, the meadows are still very wet. Snow persists above about 9,000 feet (in wet years it is much lower). Many of the lower trails are passable, how-

4

ever. The biggest hindrance is the stream crossings. Most of the larger streams are impossible to cross in June, and the smaller ones can be difficult. Even ephemeral snowmelt streams can cause difficult wades. Mosquitoes emerge in mid-June.

Despite the disadvantages, there are many nice things about June in the Teton and Washakie Wilderness Areas. The mountains are topped with white. Ephemeral waterfalls and cascades tumble down dark, volcanic walls. The landscape looks like green velvet with new growth. Wildlife is easier to see, and visitors are very scarce. Hikes 4, 5, 6, 28, 29, and 36 can usually be done by mid-June.

July
July is the driest month of the year. It is also the hottest, uncomfortably so at times. The streams are most beautiful in July. No longer in flood, they are clear and still very full. Mosquitoes are bad throughout July, and the warmer weather allows them to be active much longer at night. Mid- to late July is when the wildflowers are at their peak, and the display is astounding. Hikes 1, 2, 7, 14, 15, 16, 17, 19, 20, 21, 23, 24, 27, 32, 33, 34, 35, and 37 can usually be done by mid-July.

August
August is the most popular month for hikers. The weather is usually a bit damper than in July. Thunderstorms become more numerous, and by the end of the month, a brief snow is possible at higher elevations. Water levels recede and the fords become less onerous. All of the higher-elevation trails are accessible by early in the month, and most of the wet, marshy spots in the trails have dried up. On some hikes, lack of water becomes a serious concern when planning a trip. The mosquitoes recede in August, only to be replaced by biting flies. By the end of the month, even they are disappearing. Hikes 3, 8, 9, 10, 11, 12, 13, 18, 22, 25, 26, 30, and 31 should usually not be attempted before August 1.

September
September sees cold mornings and increasingly heavy frosts. Days vary from glorious Indian summer to quite cool. The bugs and wildflowers are gone and the aspen are turning gold. Often, new snow coats the higher elevations, making for beautiful pictures. You must be ready for cold and snow, but usually they are temporary. In many ways, September is the finest month to be in the Northern Rockies. Remember that hunting season begins in September in Wyoming, and parts of the backcountry can be very busy, including some places that see almost no summertime visitors.

Winter
The Pinyon Peak Highlands offer excellent ski touring, and opportunities abound for telemark skiing throughout the Teton and Washakie Wilderness Areas. Solitude is absolute. No one else is seen and the roar of snowmobiles should not be heard. The snowpack in this country is epic and increases as you head west.

The Teton Tornado

On July 21, 1987, the highest-elevation tornado ever recorded ripped through the Teton Wilderness. With winds gusting up to 200 miles per hour, it leveled trees along a path 20 miles long and up to 2 miles wide. The storm center passed directly over the Enos Lake area, temporarily isolating several parties of recreationists and Forest Service personnel as entire trees blew down around them.

More than 14,000 acres of the Teton Wilderness were affected, and many of the trails in the area were impassable. For the four years following the blowdown, volunteers from the American Hiking Society, Sierra Club, and Student Conservation Corps worked with the Forest Service to tear open the trails using only crosscut saws and other primitive hand tools. In August 1992, the last section of affected trail, across Two Ocean Plateau, was reopened.

Hike 6 traverses the area affected by the Teton Tornado.

HIKING THE TETON AND WASHAKIE WILDERNESS AREAS

More than 1,000 miles of trails await the adventurer in the Teton and Washakie Wilderness Areas. The precise mileage is indefinite because some trails are vague and only maintained by outfitters. About 80 percent of the trail traffic is on horses. The trails that get heavy horse use are pounded, swampy, smelly, fly-infested, and easy to follow. This book is generally not about those trails.

Trails in the Continental Divide section of the Teton Wilderness tend to be obvious and well signed. The opposite is true in the high, lonesome country of the Pinyon Peak Highlands. You can expect to spend some time holding a USGS map, puzzling over a set of faint tracks in the burn. These faint trails can be followed for many miles if you know how and are careful. Here are three rules for following the trails in the Pinyon Peak Highlands:

- First, look for blazes cut in tree trunks. Many trail routes are marked by frequent blazes. These blazes, probably first cut by Army crews in the late nineteenth century, look like upside-down exclamation points. They are usually on the oldest, and therefore, the biggest trees. Even in forests that are a mosaic of green and burned trees, many of these blazes still survive. You can use the blazes to follow a trail, even when the track or tread has disappeared completely. In fact, that's the purpose of a blaze.

- Second, with lack of use, trails disappear rapidly in a meadow. On many trails you will find that the trail disappears at each meadow. This makes it crucial to look for a blaze marking the trail when you reach the other side. In contrast, a track remains for a long time on the forest floor because grass and shrubs fill it in very slowly. Most trails vary between these two conditions, so with a little patience and resolve, you can follow these routes through the wildest country in the contiguous 48 states.

- Third, most Teton Wilderness trails follow drainages. When you lose a trail completely, as sometimes happens in completely burned areas, you can usually pick it up again by angling upslope from a stream or downslope to a stream.

The Washakie Wilderness is much drier and higher than the Teton Wilderness. In the Washakie Wilderness, most trails are fairly well marked and signed, but, because of the extensive alpine and subalpine areas that these trails traverse, many of the tracks are faint to nonexistent. These areas are marked by an elaborate system of cairns with posts sticking out of them. These lead you across miles of the remote and spectacular Absaroka and Front Range landscapes.

Sometimes the posts fall, or are infrequently placed. Binoculars help you locate these posts and can increase the quality of your experience, especially wildlife observation. In addition, your fatigue level is reduced, as you take the most direct route, cairn to cairn.

One caution: Following the cairns in a cloud can be very difficult. Loss of the route above timberline can easily cause you to "cliff-out." You should sometimes not continue because of numerous weather-related conditions on the tundra plateaus.

Following these few simple rules and suggestions, you will have no problem trekking on the trails of the Teton and Washakie Wilderness Areas to your ultimate wilderness adventure.

PLANNING YOUR TETON AND WASHAKIE WILDERNESS AREAS ADVENTURE

When you are planning a trip in the Teton and Washakie Wilderness Areas, there are four things to consider in selecting your hike (besides its length and destination).

First, what condition are the trails in? Trails in poor condition will be slower. You have to consult a map frequently, search for the track, step over logs, and walk through wet areas. Your daily mileages will reflect the trail conditions you encounter.

Second, how much elevation are you gaining? Long ascents, or trails with numerous ups and downs, take energy beyond the number of miles in the trail descriptions. In the case of passes, try to have negotiation of a pass be the only thing on the itinerary for that day.

Third, is the maximum altitude on the trip commensurate with the ability of the party and the current weather conditions? Much of the Teton and Washakie Wilderness Areas is at high altitude. Most trailheads are at least 7,000 feet, and many are higher. Some people get altitude sickness at 9,000 feet high. The temperature drops and the wind increases with altitude. The ultraviolet radiation from the sun is much more intense on the high plateaus than in drainages under the forest canopy. Dehydration and sunburn are your constant companions at high elevation. Carry at least 2 quarts of water at all times, plenty of sunblock, and lip balm. Climbing 1,000 feet on a trail that is already at 10,000 feet is harder than climbing on one that is at 8,000 feet. Frequent breaks are often necessary.

Fourth, what kind of river and stream crossings are there? Are current conditions favorable for crossing rivers and streams? Is everyone in the group comfortable with crossing swift streams and rivers? It would be frustrating to have your trip plans disrupted by an uncrossable river. It has happened to us.

Proper trip planning is key to your having the finest wilderness experience possible in the Teton and Washakie Wilderness Areas.

HOW TO USE THIS GUIDE

To use this book effectively, please note the following items:

Types of Hike

Suggested hikes have been split into the following categories:

Loop: Starts and finishes at the same trailhead, with no (or very little) retracing of your steps. Sometimes the definition of a loop is stretched to include "lollipops" and trips that involve a short walk on a road at the end of the hike to get back to your vehicle.

Shuttle: A point-to-point trip that requires two vehicles (one left at the other end of the trail), or a prearranged pickup at a designated time and place. One good way to manage the logistical problems of shuttles is to arrange for another party to start at the other end of the trail. The two parties meet at a predetermined point and then trade keys. When finished, they drive each other's vehicles home.

Out-and-back: Traveling to a specific destination, then retracing your steps back to the trailhead.

Base camp: A point-to-point hike where you spend several nights at the same campsite, using the extra days for fishing, relaxing, or day hiking.

Distances

In this guidebook, most distances are estimated. Since it's so difficult and time consuming to precisely measure trails, most distances listed in any guidebook and on trail signs are usually somebody's estimate. Keep in mind that distance is often less important than difficulty. A rocky, 2-mile, uphill trail can take longer and require more effort than 4 miles on a well-contoured trail on flat terrain.

Difficulty

To help you plan your trip, trails are rated as to difficulty. However, difficulty ratings for trails serve as a general guide only, not the final word. What is difficult to one hiker may be easy to the next. In this guidebook, difficulty ratings consider both how long and how strenuous the route is. Here are the general definitions of the ratings.

Easy: Suitable for any hiker, including children or elderly persons, without serious elevation gain, hazardous sections, or places where the trail is faint or difficult to follow.

Moderate: Suitable for hikers who have some experience and at least an average fitness level. Probably not suitable for children or the elderly unless they have an above-average level of fitness. The hike may have some short sections where the trail is difficult to follow, and often includes some hills.

Strenuous: Suitable for experienced hikers with above-average fitness level, often with sections of the trail that are difficult to follow or even some off-trail sections that could require knowledge of route-finding with a topographic map and compass, sometimes with serious elevation gain, and possibly some hazardous conditions.

Maps

The maps in this book serve as a general guide only. You definitely should take a better map with you on your hike. The maps in this guidebook do not have enough detail or do not cover enough territory.

For the Teton and Washakie Wilderness Areas, there is really only one map option—U.S. Geological Survey (USGS) quadrangle maps. The Forest Service visitor maps are reference tools only—helpful in finding the trailhead and providing the "big picture." You can usually special order any USGS quad from your local sporting goods store, or you can order them directly from the USGS at the following address:

Map Distribution
U.S. Geological Survey
Box 25286, Federal Center
Denver, CO 80225
www.usgs.gov

USGS topographic maps of the Teton and Washakie Wilderness Areas, books, and other supplies are available at these locations:

In Jackson:
   Bridger-Teton National Forest Visitor Center
   340 North Cache
   Jackson, WY 83001
   307-739-5500
   email: fbills@fs.fed.us

   Grand Teton Natural History Association
   Moose, WY 83012
   307-739-3300

   Teton Mountaineering
   170 North Cache
   Jackson, WY 83001
   307-733-3595

   Skinny Skis
   65 West Deloney Avenue
   Jackson, WY 83001
   307-733-6094

   Jack Dennis Outdoor Shop
   50 East Broadway
   Jackson, WY 83001
   307-733-3270

In Dubois:
    Shoshone National Forest
    Wind River Ranger District
    209 East Ramshorn
    Dubois, WY 82513
    307-455-2466

In Cody:
    Sunlight Sports
    1251 Sheridan Avenue
    Cody, WY 82414
    307-587-9517

    Cody Newstand
    1121 13th Street
    Cody, WY 82414
    307-587-2843

Elevation Charts
Many—but not all—hike descriptions include elevation charts. These charts don't give a detailed picture of elevation gain and loss on a hike, but they give you a general idea of how much climbing or descending you face on a trail. Hikes without elevation charts are either very short hikes or hikes without significant elevation gain or loss.

Camping
The days when guidebooks should pinpoint campsites for you are long gone. With the explosion of growth in outdoor recreation, publicizing great campsites usually leads to rapid overuse and eventual degradation that is not in keeping with the Zero Impact ethic.

Plenty of fine campsites exist in the Teton and Washakie Wilderness Areas. With just a few exceptions and proper planning, you will have no problem finding one every night. One way to ensure yourself of deluxe wilderness accomodations is to plan for your backpacking days to end in flat areas, such as river valleys or meadows. These are usually along rivers or creeks. Although many fairly flat higher-elevation campsites exist, these are much more exposed to the elements—high winds, lightning, cold, and heavy rain or summertime snow. On your USGS topo, areas where contour lines are spread apart indicate flatter ground. Many hikes in this guide refer to primitive camping. This is to assist planning and is not a substitute for familiarizing yourself with your anticipated route on USGS maps. Often these sites are not immediately obvious and require some reconnoitering to find.

Fishing
Fishing licenses are available at most convenience stores, outdoor stores, and department stores in Wyoming.

Sharing
Everybody hopes to have a wilderness all to themselves, but that rarely happens. In the Teton and Washakie Wilderness Areas, you have to share the

trails with backcountry horseriders, including large stock parties led by outfitters. If you meet a stock party on the trail, move off the trail on the uphill
side and quietly let the stock animals pass. It's too difficult (and sometimes
dangerous) for the stock animals to yield. Hikers should always yield to horses.

Backcountry Regulations

Backcountry use regulations aren't intended to complicate your life. They
help preserve the natural landscape and protect wilderness visitors. The
following backcountry use regulations pertain to the Teton and Washakie
Wilderness Areas:

In the Teton and Washakie Wilderness Areas you must:

• Suspend food at least 10 feet above the ground and 4 feet horizontally
from a post or tree.

• Carry out all trash. If you can pack it in, you can pack it out.

• Keep your group size to a maximum of 20 people.

In the Teton and Washakie Wilderness Areas you must not:

• Camp in or occupy any cabins or structures.

• Camp within 200 feet of a designated trail in the Teton Wilderness and 50
feet in the Washakie Wilderness.

• Possess or operate a motorized vehicle, any motorized equipment, bicycle,
hang glider, wheeled vehicle, or cart.

• Dispose of human waste within 100 feet of any water source, campsite, or
within sight of a trail.

• Occupy a campsite for more than 14 days. Each new campsite must be at
least 5 miles from the previous one.

• Leave a fire unattended without completely extinguishing it.

• Place or maintain a cache of gear.

• Use soaps in springs, lakes, and streams or dump waste water within 50
feet of such waters.

Zero Impact

Going into a wild area is like visiting a famous museum. You obviously do
not want to leave your mark on an art treasure in the museum. If everybody
going through the museum left one little mark, the piece of art would be
quickly destroyed—and of what value is a big building full of trashed art?
The same goes for pristine wildlands. If we all left just one little mark on the
landscape, the backcountry would soon be spoiled.

A wilderness can accommodate human use as long as everybody behaves.
But a few thoughtless or uninformed visitors can ruin it for everybody who
follows. All backcountry users have a responsibility to know and follow the
rules of Zero Impact camping.

Nowadays most wilderness users want to walk softly, but some aren't
aware that they have poor manners. Often their actions are dictated by the

outdated habits of a past generation of campers who cut green boughs for evening shelters, built campfires with fire rings, and dug trenches around tents. In the 1950s, these "camping rules" may have been acceptable. But they leave long-lasting scars, and today such behavior is absolutely unacceptable. Wild places are becoming rare, and the number of users is mushrooming. More and more camping areas show unsightly signs of heavy use.

Consequently, a new code of ethics is growing out of the necessity of coping with the unending waves of people who want a perfect backcountry experience. Today, we all must leave no clues that we were there. Enjoy the wild, but leave no indication of your visit.

THREE FALCON PRINCIPLES OF ZERO IMPACT

- Leave with everything you brought in.
- Leave no sign of your visit.
- Leave the landscape as you found it.

Most of us know better than to litter—in or out of the backcountry. Be sure you leave nothing, regardless of how small it is, along the trail or at your campsite. This means you should pack out everything, including orange peels, flip tops, cigarette butts, and gum wrappers. Also, pick up any trash that others leave behind.

Follow the main trail. Avoid cutting switchbacks and walking on vegetation beside the trail. Don't pick up "souvenirs," such as rocks, antlers, or wildflowers. The next person wants to see them, too, and collecting such souvenirs violates many regulations.

Avoid making loud noises on the trail (unless you are in bearcountry) or in camp. Be courteous—remember, sound travels easily in the backcountry, especially across water.

Carry a lightweight trowel to bury human waste 6 to 8 inches deep, at least 300 feet from any water source. Pack out used toilet paper.

Go without a campfire. Carry a stove for cooking and a flashlight, candle lantern, or headlamp for light. For emergencies, learn how to build a no-trace fire.

Camp in designated sites when they are available. Otherwise, camp and cook on durable surfaces such as bedrock, sand, gravel bars, or bare ground.

Finally, and perhaps most importantly, strictly follow the pack-in/pack-out rule. If you carry something into the backcountry, consume it or carry it out.

Put your ear to the ground and listen carefully. Thousands of people coming behind you are thanking you for your courtesy and good sense.

MAKE IT A SAFE TRIP

The Boy Scouts of America have been guided for decades by what is perhaps the single best piece of safety advice—"Be Prepared!" For starters, this

12

means carrying survival and first-aid materials, proper clothing, compass, and topographic map—and knowing how to use them.

The second-best piece of safety advice is to tell somebody where you're going and when you plan to return. Pilots must file flight plans before every trip, and anybody venturing into a blank spot on the map should do the same. File your "flight plan" with a friend or relative before taking off.

Not far behind your flight plan and being prepared with proper equipment is physical conditioning. Being fit not only makes wilderness travel more fun, it makes it safer. Here are a few more tips:

- Check the weather forecast. Be careful not to get caught at high altitude by a bad storm or along a stream in a flash flood. Watch cloud formations closely so you don't get stranded on a ridgeline during a lightning storm. Avoid traveling during prolonged periods of cold weather. Be sure your rain gear is working well—breathable fabrics degrade quickly and leak.

- The Teton and Washakie Wilderness Areas require much rugged travel at high altitude. Try to acclimatize as much as possible. Go slow, especially early in the trip. If you feel dizzy or out of sorts, sit down. If symptoms persist or worsen, return to a lower altitude.

- Avoid traveling alone in the wilderness.

- Keep your party together.

- When camping in burned areas or at their margins, choose a campsite out of range of dead or dying trees. These are at risk to fall.

- Don't camp in areas that show signs of recent landslide activity.

- The Teton and Washakie Wilderness Areas support a healthy amount of quicksand. This is particularly true in the Pinyon Peak Highlands. The authors have even encountered it on hillsides (vertical quicksand). Be careful when you encounter areas of wet sand. Test them with a stick. If the stick doesn't find bottom, walk around that area.

- Study basic survival and first aid before leaving home.

- Don't eat wild plants unless you have positively identified them.

- Before you leave for the trailhead, find out as much as you can about the route, especially the potential hazards.

- Don't exhaust yourself or other members of your party by traveling too far or too fast. Let the slowest person set the pace.

- Don't wait until you're confused to look at your maps. Follow them as you go along, from the moment you start moving up the trail, so you have a continual fix on your location.

- If you get lost, don't panic. Sit down and relax for a few minutes while you carefully check your topo map and take a reading with your compass. Confidently plan your next move. It's often smart to retrace your steps until you find familiar ground, even if you think it might lengthen your trip. Lots of people get temporarily lost in the wilderness and survive—usually by calmly and rationally dealing with the situation.

- Stay clear of all wild animals.

- Take a first-aid kit that includes, at a minimum, sewing needle, snakebite kit, aspirin, antibacterial ointment, two antiseptic swabs, two butterfly bandages, adhesive tape, four adhesive strips, four gauze pads, two triangular bandages, codeine tablets, two inflatable splints, Moleskin or Second Skin for blisters, one roll of 3-inch gauze, a CPR shield, rubber gloves, and lightweight first-aid instructions.

- Take a survival kit that includes, at a minimum, compass, whistle, matches in a waterproof container, cigarette lighter, candle, signal mirror, flashlight, fire starter, aluminum foil, water purification tablets, space blanket, and flare.

- The Teton and Washakie Wilderness Areas contain much rugged country. Heavier-weight, broken-in, all-leather boots are preferable to the ultralightweight "tennis shoe" style hiking boots.

- Have a backup plan, including maps.

- Outfitters start moving into their hunting camps on Labor Day weekend in the Teton and Washakie Wilderness Areas. By September 10, hunting season has begun. Use increases as the month progresses. You can hear the sound of gunfire. If you go hiking here in September, remember that bright orange is the universal color of safety among hunters. Wear an orange hat. Try to wear other bright colors as well, to increase your visibility. If you come upon elk gut piles or carcasses, leave the area immediately (see "Be Bear Aware"). Of course, there's always Yellowstone National Park, where hunting is prohibited.

- Last but not least, don't forget that the best defense against unexpected hazards is knowledge. Read up on the latest in wilderness safety information with Falcon's books on the subject—*Wilderness First Aid, Wilderness Survival, Reading Weather,* and *Wild Country Companion.* Check the back of this guidebook for ordering information.

Lightning: You Might Never Know What Hit You
Mountains are prone to sudden thunderstorms. If you get caught by a lightning storm, take special precautions. Remember the following:

- Lightning can travel far ahead of a storm, so be sure to take cover before the storm hits.

- Do not try to make it back to your vehicle. It isn't worth the risk. Instead, seek shelter even if it's only a short way back to the trailhead. Lightning storms usually don't last long, and from a safe vantage point, you might enjoy the sights and sounds.

- Be especially careful not to get caught on a mountaintop or exposed ridge; under large, solitary trees; in the open; or near standing water.

- Seek shelter in a low-lying area, ideally in a dense stand of small, uniformly sized trees.

- Stay away from anything that might attract lightning, such as metal tent poles, graphite fishing rods, or pack frames.

- Crouch and place both feet firmly on the ground.

- If you have a pack (without a metal frame) or a sleeping pad with you, put your feet on it for extra insulation against shock.

- Don't walk or huddle together. Instead, stay 50 feet apart, so if somebody gets hit by lightning, others in your party can give first aid.

- If you're in a tent, stay there, in your sleeping bag with your feet on your sleeping pad.

Hypothermia: The Silent Killer

Be aware of the danger of hypothermia—a condition in which the body's internal temperature drops below normal. It can lead to mental and physical collapse and death.

Hypothermia is caused by exposure to cold and is aggravated by wetness, wind, and exhaustion. The moment you begin to lose heat faster than your body produces it, you're suffering from exposure. Your body starts involuntary exercise, such as shivering, to stay warm and makes involuntary adjustments to preserve normal temperature in vital organs, restricting blood flow in the extremities. Both responses drain your energy reserves. The only way to stop the drain is to reduce the degree of exposure.

With full-blown hypothermia, as energy reserves are exhausted, cold blood reaches the brain, depriving you of good judgment and reasoning power. You won't be aware that this is happening. You lose control of your hands. Your internal temperature slides downward. Without treatment, this slide leads to stupor, collapse, and death.

To defend against hypothermia, stay dry. When clothes get wet, they lose about 90 percent of their insulating value. Wool loses relatively less heat; cotton, down, and some synthetics lose more. Choose rain clothes that cover the head, neck, body, and legs and provide good protection against wind-driven rain. Most hypothermia cases develop in air temperatures between 30 and 50 degrees F, but hypothermia can develop in warmer temperatures.

If your party is exposed to wind, cold, and wet, think hypothermia. Watch yourself and others for these symptoms: uncontrollable fits of shivering; vague, slow, slurred speech; memory lapses; incoherence; immobile, fumbling hands; frequent stumbling or a lurching gait; drowsiness (to sleep is to die); apparent exhaustion; and inability to get up after a rest. When a member of your party has hypothermia, he may deny any problem. Believe the symptoms, not the victim. Even mild symptoms demand treatment, as follows:

- Get the victim out of the wind and rain.

- Strip off all wet clothes.

- If the victim is only mildly impaired, give her warm drinks. Then get the victim in warm clothes and a warm sleeping bag. Place well-wrapped water bottles filled with heated water close to the victim.

- If the victim is badly impaired, attempt to keep him or her awake. Put the victim in a sleeping bag with another person—both naked. If you have a double bag, put two warm people in with the victim.

Fording Rivers

Perhaps more than in most national parks, the trails in the Teton and Washakie Wilderness Areas involve fords of major streams such as the Buffalo, Snake, Shoshone, Greybull, Wood, and Yellowstone Rivers. When done correctly and carefully, crossing a big river can be safe, but you must know your limits.

The most important advice is to be smart. There are cases where you simply should turn back. Even if only one member of your party (such as a child) might not be able to follow larger, stronger members, you might not want to try a risky ford. Never be embarrassed by being too cautious.

One key to safely fording rivers is confidence. If you aren't a strong swimmer, you should be. This not only allows you to safely get across a river that is a little deeper and stronger than you thought, but it gives you the confidence to avoid panic. Just like with getting lost, panic can easily make the situation worse.

Another way to build confidence is to practice. Find a warm-water river near your home and carefully practice crossing it both with a pack and without one. You can also start with a smaller stream and work up to a major river. After you've become a strong swimmer, get used to swimming in the current.

When you get to the ford, carefully assess the situation. Don't automatically cross at the point where the trail comes to the stream, heading in a straight line for the marker on the other side. A mountain river can change every spring during high runoff, so a safe ford last year might be too deep this year. Study upstream and downstream and look for a place where the stream widens and the water is not more than waist deep on the shortest member of your party. The tail end of an island is usually a good place, as is a long riffle. The inside of a meander sometimes makes a safe ford, but in other cases a long shallow section can be followed by a short, deep section next to the outside of the bend, where the current picks up speed and carves out a deep channel.

Before starting any serious ford, make sure your matches, camera, billfold, clothes, sleeping bag, and any other items you must keep dry are in watertight bags.

In the Teton and Washakie Wilderness Areas, most streams are cold, so have dry clothes ready for when you get to the other side to minimize the risk of hypothermia. This is especially true on a cold, rainy day.

Minimize the amount of time you spend in the water, but don't rush across. Instead, go slowly and deliberately, taking one step at a time, being careful to plant each foot securely before lifting the other foot. Take a 45-degree angle instead of going straight across, following a riffle line if possible.

Don't try a ford with bare feet. Wear hiking boots without the socks, sneakers, or tightly strapped sandals.

Stay sideways with the current. Turning upstream or downstream greatly increases the force of the current.

In some cases, two or three people can cross together, locking forearms with the strongest person on the upstream side.

If you have a choice, ford in the early morning when the stream isn't as deep. In the mountains, the cool evening temperatures slow snowmelt and reduce the water flow into the rivers.

On small streams, a sturdy walking stick used on the upstream side for balance helps prevent a fall, but in a major river with a fast current, a walking stick offers little help.

Loosen the belt and straps on your pack. If you fall or get washed downstream, a water-logged pack can anchor you to the bottom, so you must be able to easily release your pack. Actually, for a short period, your pack might actually help you become buoyant and float across a deep channel, but in a minute or two longer, it could become an anchor.

If you're 6'4" and a strong swimmer, you might feel secure crossing a big river, but you might have children or shorter hikers in your party. In this case, the strongest person can cross first and string a line across the river to aid those who follow. This line (with the help of a carabiner) can also be used to float packs across instead of taking a chance of a waterlogged pack dragging you under. (If you knew about the ford in advance, you could pack along a lightweight rubber raft or inner tube for this purpose.) Depending on their size and strength, you might also want to carry children.

Be prepared for the worst. Sometimes circumstances can arise where you simply must cross instead of going back, even though the ford looks dangerous. Also, you can underestimate the depth of the channel or strength of the current, especially after a thunderstorm when a muddy river hides its true depth. In these cases, whether you like it or not, you might be swimming.

It's certainly recommended to avoid these situations, but if they happen, be prepared. The first rule is do not panic. The second rule is do not try to swim directly across. Instead, pick a long angle and gradually cross to the other side, taking as much as 100 yards or more to finally get across. If your pack starts to drag you down, get out of it immediately, even if you have to abandon it. If you lose control and get washed downstream, go feet first, so you don't hit your head on rocks or logs.

And finally, be sure to report any dangerous ford to a ranger as soon as you finish your trip. Hikes 3, 4, 9, 10, 11, 16, 19, 21, 22, 29, 30, 32, and 37 include serious fords.

EMERGENCY MEDICAL SERVICES

In case of emergency, dial 911, just like in the big city. You can find comprehensive medical services at West Park Hospital in Cody, Wyoming, and at St. John's Hospital in Jackson, Wyoming.

BE BEAR AWARE

The first step of any hike in bear country is an attitude adjustment. Nothing guarantees total safety. Hiking in bear country like Teton and Washakie Wilderness Areas adds a small additional risk to your trip. However, that risk can be greatly minimized by adhering to this age-old piece of advice— be prepared. And being prepared doesn't only mean having the right equipment. It also means having the right information. Knowledge is your best defense.

You can—and should—thoroughly enjoy your trip to bear country. Don't let the fear of bears ruin your vacation. This fear can accompany you every step of the way. It can constantly lurk in the back of your mind, preventing you from enjoying the wildest and most beautiful places left on earth. And even worse, some bear experts think bears might actually be able to sense your fear.

Being prepared and being knowledgeable gives you confidence. It allows you to fight back the fear that can burden you throughout your stay in bear country. You won't—nor should you—forget about bears and the basic rules of safety, but proper preparation allows you to keep the fear of bears at bay and let enjoyment rule the day.

And on top of that, do we really want to be totally safe? If we did, we probably would never go hiking in the wilderness—bears or no bears. We certainly wouldn't, at much greater risk, drive hundreds of miles to get to the trailhead. Perhaps a tinge of danger adds a desired element to our wilderness trip.

Hiking In Bear Country

Nobody likes surprises, and bears dislike them, too. The majority of bear maulings occur when a hiker surprises a bear. Therefore, it's vital to do everything possible to avoid these surprise meetings. Perhaps the best way is to know the five-part system. If you follow these five rules, the chance of encountering a bear on the trail sink to the slimmest possible margin.

- Be alert.
- Go in with a group and stay together.
- Stay on the trail.
- Hike in the middle of the day.
- Make noise.

No substitute for alertness: As you hike, watch ahead and to the sides. Don't fall into the all-too-common and particularly nasty habit of fixating on the trail 10 feet ahead. It's especially easy to do this when dragging a heavy pack up a long hill or when carefully watching your step on a heavily eroded trail.

Using your knowledge of bear habitat and habits, be especially alert in areas most likely to be frequented by bears such as avalanche chutes, berry patches, along streams, through stands of whitebark pine, etc.

Watch carefully for bear sign and be especially watchful (and noisy) if you see any. If you see a track or a scat, but it doesn't look fresh, pretend it is. This area is obviously frequented by bears.

Watch the wind: The wind can be a friend or foe. The strength and direction of the wind can make a significant difference in your chances of an encounter with a bear. When the wind is blowing at your back, your smell travels ahead of you, alerting any bear that might be on or near the trail ahead. Conversely, when the wind blows in your face, your chances of a surprise meeting with a bear increase, so make more noise and be more alert.

A strong wind can also be noisy and limit a bear's ability to hear you coming. If a bear can't smell or hear you coming, the chances of an encounter greatly increase, so watch the wind.

Safety in numbers: There have been very few instances where a large group has had an encounter with a bear. On the other hand, a large percentage of hikers mauled by bears were hiking alone. Large groups naturally make more noise and put out more smell and probably appear more threatening to bears. In addition, if you're hiking alone and get injured, there is nobody to go for help. For these reasons, rangers in Yellowstone recommend parties of four or more hikers when going into bear country.

If the large party splits up, it becomes two small groups, and the advantage is lost, so stay together. If you're on a family hike, keep the kids from running ahead. If you're in a large group, keep the stronger members from going ahead or weaker members from lagging behind. The best way to prevent this natural separation is to ask one of the slowest members of the group to lead. This keeps everybody together.

Stay on the trail: Although bears use trails, they don't often use them during midday when hikers commonly use them. Through generations of associating trails with people, bears probably expect to find hikers on trails, especially during midday.

Contrarily, bears probably don't expect to find hikers off trails. Bears rarely settle down in a day bed right along a heavily used trail. However, if you wander around in thickets off the trail, you are more likely to stumble into an occupied day bed or cross paths with a traveling bear.

Sleeping late: Bears—and most other wildlife—usually aren't active during the middle of the day, especially on a hot summer day. Wild animals are most active around dawn and dusk. Therefore, hiking early in the morning or late afternoon increases your chances of seeing wildlife, including bears. Likewise, hiking during midday on a hot August day greatly reduces the chance of an encounter.

Sounds: Perhaps the best way to avoid a surprise meeting with a bear is to make sure the bear knows you're coming, so make lots of noise. Some experts think metallic noise is superior to human voices, which can be muffled by natural conditions, but the important issue is making lots of noise, regardless of what kind of noise.

Running: Many avid runners like to get off paved roads and running tracks and onto backcountry trails. But running on trails in bear country can be seriously hazardous to your health.

Leave the night to the bears: Like running on trails, hiking at night can be very risky. Bears are more active after dark, and you can't see them until it's too late. If you get caught at night, be sure to make lots of noise, and remember that bears commonly travel on hiking trails at night.

You can be dead meat, too: If you see or smell a carcass of a dead animal when hiking, immediately vacate the area. Don't let your curiosity keep you near the carcass a second longer than necessary. Bears commonly hang around a carcass, guarding it and feeding on it for days until it's completely consumed. Your presence could easily be interpreted as a threat to the bear's food supply, and a vicious attack could be imminent.

If you see a carcass ahead of you on the trail, don't go any closer. Instead, abandon your hike and return to the trailhead. If the carcass is between you and the trailhead, take a very long detour around it, upwind from the carcass, making lots of noise along the way. Be sure to report the carcass to the local ranger. This might prompt a temporary trail closure or special warnings and prevent injury to other hikers. Rangers will, in some cases, go in and drag the carcass away from the trail.

Cute, cuddly, and lethal: If you see a bear cub, don't go one inch closer to it. It might seem abandoned, but it most likely is not. Mother bear is probably very close, and female bears fiercely defend their young.

It doesn't do you any good in your pack: If you brought a repellent such as pepper spray, don't bury it in your pack. Keep it as accessible as possible. Most pepper spray comes in a holster or somehow conveniently attaches to your belt or pack. Such protection won't do you any good if you can't have it ready to fire in one or two seconds. Before hitting the trail, read the directions carefully and test fire the spray.

Regulations: Nobody likes rules and regulations. However, national parks have a few that you must follow. These rules aren't meant to take the freedom out of your trip. They are meant to help bring you back safely.

But I didn't see any bears: Now you know how to be safe. Walk up the trail constantly clanging two metal pans together. It works every time. You won't see a bear, but you'll hate your "wilderness experience." You left the city to get away from loud noise.

Yes, you can be very safe, but how safe do you want to be and still be able to enjoy your trip? It's a balancing act. First, be knowledgeable and then decide how far you want to go. Everybody has to make his or her own personal choice.

Here's another conflict. If you do everything listed here, you most likely will not see any bears—or any deer or moose or eagles or any other wildlife. Again, you make the choice. If you want to be as safe as possible, follow these rules religiously. If you want to see wildlife, including bears, do all of this in reverse, but then you are increasing your chance of an encounter instead of decreasing it.

Camping In Bear Country

Staying overnight in bear country is not dangerous, but it adds a slight additional risk to your trip. The main difference is the presence of more food, cooking, and garbage. Plus, you are in bear country at night when bears are usually most active. Once again, however, following a few basic rules greatly minimizes this risk.

Storing food and garbage: If the campsite doesn't have a bear-proof storage box or bear pole, be sure to set one up or at least locate one before it gets dark. It's not only difficult to store food after darkness falls, but it's easier to forget some juicy morsel on the ground. Also, be sure to store food in airtight, waterproof bags to prevent food odors from circulating throughout the forest. For double protection, put food and garbage in zip-locked bags and then seal tightly in a larger plastic bag.

The following illustrations depict three popular methods for hanging food bags. In any case, try to get food and garbage at least 10 feet off the ground.

Special equipment: They're not really that special, but you definitely should have a good supply of zip-locked bags. This handy invention is perfect for keeping food smell to a minimum and helps keep food from spilling on your pack, clothing, or other gear.

Take a special bag for storing food. The bag must be sturdy and waterproof. You can get dry bags at most outdoor specialty stores, but you can get by with a trash compactor bag. Regular garbage bags can break and leave your food spread on the ground.

You also need 100 feet of nylon cord. You don't need a heavy climbing rope to store food. Go light instead. Parachute cord will usually suffice unless you plan to hang large quantities of food and gear (which might be the case on a long backpacking excursion with a large group).

You can also buy a small pulley system to make hoisting a heavy load easier. Again, you can usually get by without this extra weight in your pack unless you have a massive load to hang.

What to hang: To be as safe as possible, store everything that has any food smell. This includes cooking gear, eating utensils, bags used to keep food in your pack, all garbage, and even clothes with food smells on them. If you spilled something on your clothes, change into other clothes for sleeping and hang clothes with food smells with the food and garbage. If you take them into the tent, you aren't separating your sleeping area from food smells. Try to keep food odors off your pack, but if you failed, put the food bag inside and hang the pack.

What to keep in your tent: You can't be too careful in keeping food smells out of the tent. Just in case a bear has become accustomed to coming into that campsite looking for food, it's vital to keep all food smells out of the tent. This often includes your pack, which is hard to keep odor free. Usually only take valuables (like cameras and binoculars), clothing, and sleeping gear into the tent.

If you brought a bear repellent such as pepper spray, sleep with it. Also, keep a flashlight in the tent. If an animal comes into camp and wakes you up, you need the flashlight to identify it.

The campfire: Regulations prohibit campfires in most campsites in Teton and Washakie Wilderness Areas, but if you're in an area where fires are allowed, treat yourself. Besides adding the nightly entertainment, the fire might make your camp safer from bears.

The campfire provides the best possible way to get rid of food smells. Build a small but hot fire and thoroughly burn everything that smells of food—garbage, leftovers, fish entrails, everything. If you brought food in cans or other incombustible containers, burn them, too. You can even dump extra water from cooking or dishwater on the edge of the fire to erase the smell.

Be very sure you have the fire hot enough to completely burn everything. If you leave partially burned food scraps in the fire, you are setting up a dangerous situation for the next camper using this site.

Before leaving camp the next morning, dig out the fire pit and pack out anything that has not completely burned, even if you believe it no longer carries food smells. For example, many foods like dried soup or hot chocolate come in foil packages that might seem like they burn, but they really don't. Pack out the scorched foil and cans (now with very minor food smells). Also pack out foil and cans left by other campers.

Types of food: Don't get paranoid about the types of food you bring. All food has some smell, and you can make your trip much less enjoyable by fretting too much over food. *What* food you have along is much less critical than *how* you handle it, cook it, and store it. A can of tuna fish might put out a smell, but if you eat all of it in one meal, don't spill it on the ground or on your clothes, and burn the can later, it can be quite safe.

Perhaps the safest option is freeze-dried food. It carries very little smell, and it comes in convenient envelopes that allow you to "cook it" by merely adding boiling water. This means you don't have cooking pans to wash or store. However, freeze-dried food is very expensive, and many backpackers don't use it—but still safely enjoy bear country. Dry, prepacked meals (often pasta- or rice-based) offer an affordable compromise to freeze-dried foods.

Hanging food at night is not the only storage issue. Also make sure you place food correctly in your pack. Use airtight packages as much as possible. Store food in the containers it came in or, when opened, in zip-locked bags. This keeps food smells out of your pack and off your other camping gear and clothes.

How to cook: The overriding philosophy of cooking in bear country is to create as little odor as possible. Keep it simple. Use as few pans and dishes as possible.

Unless it's a weather emergency, don't cook in the tent. If you like winter backpacking, you probably cook in the tent, but you should have a different tent for summer backpacking.

If you can have a campfire and decide to cook fish, try cooking them in aluminum foil envelopes instead of frying them. Then, after removing the cooked fish, quickly and completely burn the fish scraps off the foil. Using foil also means you don't have to wash the pan you used to cook the fish.

Be careful not to spill on yourself while cooking. If you do, change clothes and hang the clothes with food odor with the food and garbage. Wash your hands thoroughly before retiring to the tent.

Don't cook too much food, so you don't have to deal with leftovers. If you do end up with extra food, however, you only have two choices: Carry it out or burn it. Don't bury it or throw it in a lake or leave it anywhere in bear country. A bear will most likely find and dig up any food or garbage buried in the backcountry.

Taking out the garbage: Prepare for garbage problems before you leave home. Bring along airtight zip-locked bags to store garbage. Be sure to hang your garbage at night along with your food. Also, carry in as little garbage as possible by discarding excess packaging while packing.

Washing dishes: This is a sticky problem, but there is one easy solution. If you don't dirty dishes, you don't have to wash them. So try to minimize food smell by using as few dishes and pans as possible. If you use the principles of no-trace camping, you are probably doing as much as you can to reduce food smell from dishes.

If you brought paper towels, use one to carefully remove food scraps from pans and dishes before washing them. Then, when you wash dishes, you have much less food smell. Burn the dirty towels or store them in zip-locked bags with other garbage. Put pans and dishes in zip-locked bags before putting them back in your pack.

If you end up with lots of food scraps in the dishwater, drain out the scraps and store them in zip-locked bags with other garbage or burn them. You can bring a lightweight screen to filter out food scraps from dishwater, but be sure to store the screen with the food and garbage. If you have a campfire, pour the dishwater around the edge of the fire. If you don't have a fire, take the dishwater at least 200 feet downwind and downhill from camp and pour it on the ground or in a small hole. Don't put dishwater or food scraps in a lake or stream.

Although possibly counter to accepted rules of cleanliness for many people, you can skip washing dishes altogether on the last night of your trip. Instead, simply use the paper towels to clean the dirty dishes as much as possible. You can wash them when you get home. Pack dirty dishes in zip-locked bags before putting them back in your pack.

Finally, don't put it off. Do dishes immediately after eating, so a minimum of food smell lingers in the area.

Choosing a tent site: Try to keep your tent site at least 100 feet from your cooking area. In the Teton and Washakie Wilderness Areas, unfortunately, some campsites do not adequately separate the cooking area from the tent site. Store food at least 100 yards from the tent. You can store it near the cooking area to further concentrate food smells.

Not under the stars: Some people prefer to sleep out under the stars instead of using a tent. This might be okay in areas not frequented by bears, but it's not a good idea in bear country. The thin fabric of a tent certainly isn't any real physical protection from a bear, but it does present a psychological barrier to a bear that wants to come even closer.

Do somebody a big favor: Report all bear sightings to the ranger after your trip. This might not help *you,* but it could save another camper's life. If rangers get enough reports to spot a pattern, they manage the area to prevent potentially hazardous situations.

The Bear Essentials of Hiking and Camping

- Knowledge is the best defense.
- There is no substitute for alertness.
- Hike with a large group and stay together.
- Don't hike alone in bear country.
- Stay on the trail.
- Hike in the middle of the day.
- Make lots of noise while hiking.
- Never approach a bear.
- Females with cubs are very dangerous.
- Stay away from carcasses.
- Defensive hiking works. Try it.
- Choose a safe campsite.
- Camp below timberline.
- Separate sleeping and cooking areas.
- Sleep in a tent.
- Cook just the right amount of food and eat it all.
- Store food and garbage out of reach of bears.
- Never feed bears.
- Keep food odors out of the tent.
- Leave the campsite cleaner than you found it.
- Leave no food rewards for bears.

BE MOUNTAIN LION ALERT

The most important safety element for recreation in mountain lion country is simply recognizing their habitat. Mountain lions primarily feed on deer, so these common ungulates are a key element in cougar habitat. Fish and wildlife agencies usually have good information about deer distribution from population surveys and hunting results. Where you have a high deer population, you can expect to find mountain lions.

Deer tracks can be found easily on dirt roads and trails. If you are not familiar with identifying deer tracks, seek the advice of someone knowledgeable, or refer to a book on animal tracks such as Falcon's *Scats and Tracks* series.

Safety guidelines for traveling in mountain lion country: To stay as safe as possible when hiking in mountain lion country, follow this advice:

• Travel with a friend or group. There's safety in numbers, so stay together.

• Don't let small children wander away by themselves.

• Don't let pets run unleashed.

• Avoid hiking at dawn and dusk—the times mountain lions are most active.

• Know how to behave if you encounter a mountain lion.

What to do if you encounter a mountain lion: In the vast majority of mountain lion encounters, these animals exhibit avoidance, indifference, or curiosity that never result in human injury. But it is natural to be alarmed if you have an encounter of any kind. Try to keep your cool and consider the following:

Recognize threatening mountain lion behavior. A few cues may help you gauge the risk of attack. If a mountain lion is more than 50 yards away, and it directs its attention to you, it may be only curious. This situation represents only a slight risk for adults, but a more serious risk to unaccompanied children. At this point, you should move away, while keeping the animal in your peripheral vision. Also, look for rocks, sticks, or something to use as a weapon, just in case.

If a mountain lion is crouched and staring intensely at you less than 50 yards away, it may be assessing the chances of a successful attack. If this behavior continues, the risk of attack may be high.

Do not approach a mountain lion. Instead, give the animal the opportunity to move on. Slowly back away, but maintain eye contact if close. Mountain lions are not known to attack humans to defend young or a kill, but they have been reported to "charge" in rare instances and may want to stay in the area. It's best to choose another route or time to hike through the area.

Do not run from a mountain lion. Running may stimulate a predatory response.

Make noise. If you encounter a mountain lion, be vocal and talk or yell loudly and regularly. Try not to panic. Shout in a way that others in the area are made aware of the situation.

Maintain eye contact. Eye contact presents a challenge to the mountain lion, showing you are aware of its presence. Eye contact also helps you know where it is. However, if the behavior of the mountain lion is not threatening (if it is, for example, grooming or periodically looking away), maintain visual contact through your peripheral vision and move away.

Appear larger than you are. Raise your arms above your head and make steady waving motions. Raise your jacket or another object above your head. Do not bend over, as this will make you appear smaller and more "prey-like."

If you are with small children, pick them up. First, bring children close to you, maintain eye contact with the mountain lion, and pull the children up without bending over. If you are with other children or adults, band together.

Defend yourself. If attacked, fight back. Try to remain standing. Do not feign death. Pick up a branch or rock; pull out a knife, pepper spray, or other deterrent device. Remember that everything is a potential weapon, and individuals have fended off mountain lions with blows from rocks, tree limbs, and even cameras.

Defend others. Defend your hiking partners, but don't defend your pet. In past attacks on children, adults have successfully stopped attacks. However, such cases are very dangerous and risky, and physically defending a pet is not recommended.

Respect any warning signs posted by agencies.

Spread the word. Before leaving on your hike, discuss lions and teach others in your group how to behave in case of a mountain lion encounter. For example, anyone who starts running could bring on an attack.

Report encounters. If you have an encounter with a mountain lion, record your location and the details of the encounter, and notify the nearest landowner or land-managing agency. The land management agency (federal, state, or county) may want to visit the site and, if appropriate, post education/warning signs. Fish and wildlife agencies should also be notified because they record and track such encounters.

If physical injury occurs, it is important to leave the area and not disturb the site of attack. Mountain lions that have attacked people must be killed, and an undisturbed site is critical for effectively locating the dangerous mountain lion.

See Falcon's *Mountain Lion Alert* for more details and tips for safe outdoor recreation in mountain lion country.

AVALANCHE SAFETY

Anyone who ventures into the hills or mountains when snow blankets the ground should first read *The Avalanche Book* by Betsy Armstrong and Knox Williams (1986, Fulcrum Publishing, Inc., 350 Indiana Street #350, Golden, Colorado, 80401, 800-992-9208). The authors are veterans of avalanche research and education, and the book drives home its lessons with riveting narratives about real-life avalanches and their victims. At the very least, the book will motivate anyone who sets out for the snowy hills to first enroll in an avalanche safety course. The only way to travel safely in avalanche terrain is to learn firsthand from experts how to evaluate the risks.

Armstrong and Williams estimate that, in the United States, some 100,000 avalanches occur every year. On average, 100 of these cause injury, death, or destruction to property. About 140 people a year (again, looking at averages) are caught in avalanches; 17 of them are killed. Canada averages 7 avalanche victims a year. In the United States since 1950, fully 75 percent of avalanche victims were recreationists. Undoubtedly, as more people head for the hills during avalanche season, the number of fatalities will increase.

The recipe for avalanche is simple: snow and slope. Slides can happen on any slope but are most common on slopes of between 30 to 50 degrees. Exceptions can be deadly. According to Armstrong and Williams, one wet-snow slide released on a beginners slope at a ski area in Japan, killing seven people. The slope angle was only 10 degrees.

To better evaluate avalanche risk, it helps to understand how snowflakes behave when they gang up together. As snow falls, it accumulates on the ground in layers collectively called the snowpack. Some layers are made up of loose, sugary snow; other layers, composed of rounded and tightly packed crystals, are more solid and cohesive. Sun, wind, and surface thawing and freezing add hard or brittle crusts to the snowpack's profile. Some layers are thick, some thin.

Temperature plays an important role in a developing snowpack. The snowpack is usually warmest near the ground, and coldest just beneath the surface of the snow. This difference in temperature is called the temperature gradient (TG, in the lingo). A wide spread of temperatures (a high temperature gradient) causes TG crystals or depth hoar to form. TG crystals bond together poorly. Grab a handful of TG crystals and the stuff drains between your fingers like coarse sugar. A TG layer often forms at the base of a snowpack, acting like a sheet of ball bearings for the layers above. A low temperature gradient allows snow crystals to bond together, forming a stronger, cohesive layer. This layer, or slab, on top of a TG layer means a higher risk of avalanche.

Generally, the snowpack changes very slowly in sustained sub-zero cold. But from 20 degrees F to near freezing, the snowpack settles rapidly and bonds will form between grains of snow. At temperatures warmer than freezing (32 degrees F), the snowpack settles densely onto itself and begins to thaw. A thaw, particularly in the spring, produces wet-snow avalanches and is the second most common cause of avalanches.

Avalanches come in two forms: loose and slab. A loose slide typically starts at a single point and fans out as it travels downhill. Loose slides usually involve fairly dry snow near the surface of the snowpack. A slab avalanche occurs when a strongly bonded layer (usually resting atop a weaker layer) breaks all at once across a wide area, and the entire layer, or slab, slides downhill. Dangerous slabs can form due to wind or sun crusts, thawing and consolidation of a surface layer, or when relatively warm, dense snow settles on a weak, loose layer.

Tools

For any outing into avalanche terrain, always pack along a few essential tools of the trade. Carry a shovel. Several lightweight, compact models are available with telescoping handles or folding blades. The shovel must be stiff, strong, and durable. New snow is easy to dig through, but when an avalanche stops, its load of snow sets up like concrete. You can also use the shovel to dig snow analysis pits and shelters.

Rescue beacons or transceivers are proven time—and life—savers when searching for buried avalanche victims. These small radio transmitters and receivers send a signal allowing survivors (wearing transceivers) to home in on the victim. Transceivers are costly (around $225 apiece), and require training and regular practice. You must have at least two—one to receive the other's signal—and ideally everyone in the group should wear a transceiver.

Evaluating Avalanche Risk

Perhaps the most important fact to remember when weighing avalanche risk is that 80 percent of all avalanches occur during or just after fresh snowfall. The hazard is highest when snow accumulates at a rate of 1 inch per hour or more. And large slides—big enough to kill—are most likely when 1 foot or more of snow is added to the snowpack: the more snow, the bigger the potential slide. Wind generally increases the avalanche risk. Wind-deposited snow is more dense and heavier than fresh snow, and when loaded onto leeward slopes it adds weight and stress to the snowpack. Armstrong and Williams warn that "wind can turn a 1-foot snowfall into a 300-foot drift in a starting zone."

With this said, the first step everyone should take before heading into the hills is obvious: look out the window at the weather and check the forecast. Also consider the effect on the snowpack of recent weather—last week's snowfall, yesterday's winds, and temperature patterns through the winter. Call the avalanche report for the area you plan to visit; look in the phone book under U.S. Government—USDA Forest Service. Heed their advice.

As you travel across the snow, stay alert for signs of avalanche danger. Look for evidence of recent slides. Think about the snow you're traveling on. Is there an obvious crust or slab? Is it strong ("Will it support my weight"), or weak ("Do I break through now and then")? Watch for cracks radiating out from your skis. Listen for hollow noises underfoot. Does the snow settle all at once in a wide area as you travel on it? All these factors indicate a dangerous slab.

Also consider the layers beneath the surface. You can take a rough survey of layers within the snowpack by poking a ski pole down through the snow, feeling for crusts, air pockets, and dense or loose layers. But the best way to test the snowpack is to dig a quick snow pit. Once again, a course in avalanche safety is invaluable. You can learn the basics of how to dig a snowpit from a book, but only hands-on experience—with an avalanche expert explaining each step—will teach you how to interpret the nuances of the snowpack revealed in the wall of the pit.

Remember that snow pits are not foolproof; interpreting the clues of a pit requires intuition built on years of experience. Dig a pit whenever you get the chance—start acquiring that experience. It also helps to dig more than one pit (in another part of the slope) to compare findings. If the evidence is unclear, avoid the slope and live to try it again some other day. And regardless of what the pit indicates, stay alert to other signs of avalanche risk.

Also look carefully at the terrain. Steep bowls and gullies are obvious slide zones. Look for suspicious clearings between trees, or trees stripped of branches on one side, leaning downhill. Stay off slopes of 30 degrees or more. Dangle a ski pole like a plumb line to eye the angle of a slope.

A slope does not have to be long or broad to slide. Even small pitches can slide. And previous ski or snowmobile tracks do not indicate a safe slope. The snow may slide on the second person to cross it, or the third, or fifteenth.

Remember that even slopes covered with trees can avalanche. If the trees are spaced widely enough to allow downhill skiing, then they do not provide enough of an anchor to prevent a slide.

To find a route around an avalanche track, either stay above the starting zone or below and far away from runouts. Generally the best route is on windward sides near tops of ridges. Avoid cornices. Even road cuts can be dangerous; a slide may start on the slope above and drop onto someone below. Consider the risks: What's the worst that could happen? Are there safe havens or possible escape routes? Where would I end up if this slope slides?

Choose campsites well away from starting zones, tracks, and runouts. Also, don't travel alone in avalanche terrain. When traversing suspect terrain, loosen your pack straps, put on a hat, gloves, and goggles, and zip up your jacket—anything to seal out snow and cold. Remove ski straps. Turn your transceiver on if wearing one. Expose only one person at a time to risk. Others in the group should remain in the shelter of trees or well above or to the sides of the slope. Watch each traveler until he or she is safe—if the slope does slide, you'll have a better idea of where to look for the victim. Don't pause in the middle of an avalanche slope; minimize the amount of time you are exposed to risk.

If You are Caught in an Avalanche

Try to reach the side of the slide and swim toward the surface. As the slide slows, swim with all your effort toward the top, bring your hands in front of your face, and try to create breathing room around your head and chest before the snow stops and sets up. Then relax. Try to remain calm, breathing slowly. Conserve oxygen. Yell only if you hear rescuers approaching. Try to wiggle anything free that might be near or above the surface to attract attention. It's nearly impossible to dig yourself out, even if buried only 1 foot deep. One avalanche survivor likened it to being encased in a giant body cast. Buried more than 2 feet deep, you've got a fifty-fifty chance of survival. The deeper you are, the worse are your chances. Only half the victims buried for longer than 30 minutes survive. In the backcountry, when additional help is far away, it's up to your companions to dig you out. . .fast.

Rescuers looking for a buried person should consider the risk of another slide before rushing to help. Post a sentry if another slide is possible and you can spare the manpower. Then, if it's safe to do so, mark the spot where the person was last seen. If you're wearing transceivers, make sure everyone switches to receive. Search the fall line below the last-seen mark for clues—clothing, equipment, a foot or hand poking out of the snow, even a smear of blood—anything to lead to the person. Look for likely pockets where a person might have hung up—near trees, boulders, in snow-filled hollows. Armstrong and Williams report that many victims are found right at the toe of the debris in the runout zone. Use ski poles or a probe pole to feel for a body or gear. Kick at the surface with your boots to dislodge chunks of snow. Keep looking. Remember, each passing minute reduces the person's chance of survival.

If you find the victim, check breathing and pulse. Look for plugs of snow in the mouth and nose and remove them. Check for bleeding, broken bones, internal injuries. Treat for shock and hypothermia as needed.

Finally, heed the advice of Armstrong and Williams. "Avoiding avalanches is easier than surviving them."

For more information on avalanche safety, see *Avalanche Aware* and *Wild Country Companion*, both by Falcon Publishing, Inc.

Pinyon Peak Highlands

1 Huckleberry Ridge

> **Highlights:** A lookout tower with a spectacular view of the Tetons and Jackson Lake.
> **Type of hike:** Out-and-back day hike or backpack.
> **Total distance:** 12 miles.
> **Difficulty:** Moderate.
> **Maps:** USGS Flagg Ranch and Huckleberry Ridge quads; Bridger-Teton National Forest map, Buffalo and Jackson Ranger Districts.

Finding the trailhead: Called the Sheffield Creek Trail on the maps, but the Huckleberry Ridge Trail on the trail signs, this trailhead is reached by turning onto a dirt road on the east side of U.S. Highway 89/191/287, just 2.7 miles south of the south entrance to Yellowstone National Park and 25 miles north of Moran Junction. This dirt road is immediately south of the highway bridge spanning the Snake River at the busy Flagg Ranch. The road ends after 0.4 mile at a signed trailhead immediately beyond a stream crossing. If the stream is too high, park at a small lot 0.1 mile before it.

Parking and trailhead facilities: Busy Sheffield Creek Campground (fee) is near the trailhead but has only five sites. It has outhouses, picnic tables, bear-proof refuse containers, and potable water. Contact the Bridger-Teton National Forest for reservations.

Key Points:
- 3.0 Sheffield Creek
- 4.0 Top of Huckleberry Ridge
- 6.0 Huckleberry Mountain Lookout

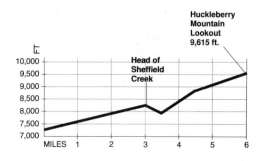

32

On Huckleberry Ridge. LEE MERCER PHOTO

The hike: The Huck Fire was ignited by a downed electrical wire just across the road at Flagg Ranch on Labor Day weekend 1988. You will be in the burn until you reach the top of Huckleberry Ridge, a nearly continuous climb of 2,200 feet. For this reason, it is essential to start early, as there is no shade available in the burn. Carry plenty of water for the climb.

From the signed trailhead, bear right across a small meadow and begin the ascent. The trail climbs through a scorched forest for 1,600 feet without a break. The fire burned very intensely through here. At 3 miles, you finally reach a short descent across the head of Sheffield Creek, where you leave the burn and enter a beautiful forest of whitebark pine, Douglas-fir, and subalpine fir.

After the short descent, you begin a climb of 600 more feet, passing through scattered open forest with a beautiful view of the northern portion of the Teton Range. You reach the top at 4 miles and 9,200 feet. The Tetons lie before you to the west and southwest. To the northwest is the flat, forested, and wild Pitchstone Plateau in Yellowstone National Park, formed just yesterday (in geological time) by vast outpourings of lava. Snowdrifts linger on the 7-mile-long top of Huckleberry Ridge until mid-July. Winter storms leave more than 300 inches of snow here per year. But, by mid-August, the tributaries of Sheffield Creek are mostly dry.

At 5.5 miles you reach a sign that says, "Lookout." No trail is immediately obvious. Walk directly toward the low spot on the ridge, where there is a small spring in wet years. From here, pick up the trail, which is very distinct once you find it. Hike up a very steep series of switchbacks that

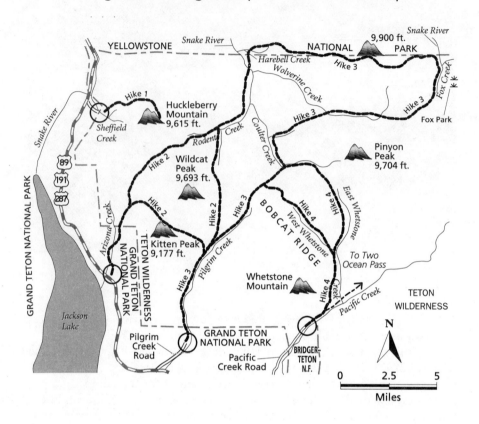

climb 500 feet in 0.5 mile to the lookout. From here the view of the Tetons and Jackson Lake is spellbinding. All of the Teton Wilderness is visible, with the Continental Divide appearing as a vast and impenetrable wall at the border with the Washakie Wilderness, many miles east of where you stand. To the south is Mount Leidy, the Gros Ventre Range, and the distant icy summits of the Wind River Range. Looking north, Mount Sheridan, Two Ocean Plateau, the great valley of the Snake River, and the volcanic Red Hills, including Heart Lake, anchor the great wild country south of Yellowstone Lake, in Yellowstone National Park.

Retrace your steps back to your rig.

2 Kitten Ridge Loop

See Map on Page 34

Highlights: A moderate trip through some of the least-traveled backcountry in the contiguous 48 states; numerous meadows, ponds, and wildlife. Superlative views from Kitten Ridge.
Type of hike: Backpacking loop.
Total distance: 29.5 miles.
Difficulty: Strenuous.
Maps: USGS Colter Bay, Flagg Ranch, Huckleberry Ridge, and Two Ocean Lake quads; Bridger-Teton National Forest map, Buffalo and Jackson Ranger Districts.

Finding the trailhead: From Moran, Wyoming, head north on U.S. Highway 89/191/287 for 13.4 miles to the unsigned Arizona Creek Trailhead, which is a short distance off US 89/287 on your right. Turn right (east) onto an obscure dirt road at a point immediately north of the unsigned highway bridge over Arizona Creek. The turnoff is 4.8 miles north of the road to Colter Bay Village and hard to see. Be alert or you will surely miss it. The dirt road ends in 100 yards at a corral.

Parking and trailhead facilities: This trailhead is in Grand Teton National Park. Teton Wilderness users can park overnight. No camping is allowed at the trailhead.

Key points:
1.5 Teton Wilderness boundary.
4.0 Bailey Meadows.
8.0 Kitten Ridge.
12.0 Junction with Pilgrim Creek Trail.
12.3 Junction with East Rodent Trail.
16.3 Wildcat Ridge.
20.0 Junction with Rodent Creek Trail.
22.0 Brown Meadows.

The hike: Were it not for the occasional noise of airplanes you could imagine civilization had disappeared. This hike is one of the wildest and least traveled described in this book. The burned trees resembling ghostly apparitions

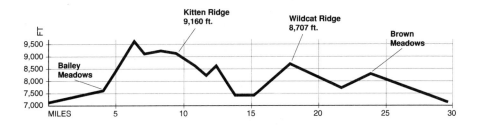

and the specter of the grizzly bear, wolf, and wolverine create an unforgettable wilderness experience for those few who venture here.

The Arizona Creek Trail begins left (north) of the corral. Note that both the Colter Bay quad and the Bridger-Teton National Forest map show a primitive road going up Arizona Creek for about 1 mile. The road has been closed for quite some time and is rapidly reverting to nature. The trail, although faint, is easy to follow. It winds through a short stretch of lodgepole pine, then breaks into a meadow. The meadow is large and pleasant, but the noise of highway traffic intrudes, as do the powerlines toward which the trail heads and passes under. Past the powerlines, you climb through aspen and into a thick stand of lodgepole pine as you cross over a hill and drop slowly to Arizona Creek. The sounds of the machine culture fade— deep wilderness lies ahead.

Within 0.5 mile, you reach an impressive wall of willows lining Arizona Creek. At 0.7 mile, the willows open up into a real meadow. One hundred yards beyond it, the trail crosses Arizona Creek. After just another 100 yards, the trail enters another small meadow with a good view of the Tetons behind you. At 1.5 miles, you pass the wilderness boundary and enter the Teton Wilderness. You're already in wild country and headed for wilder.

At 1.7 miles, the trail starts to climb noticeably. It will gain 700 feet between here and Bailey Meadows. The trail forks at 2.3 miles. Bear right and continue uphill. Now the trail peters out to nothing more than an erosion ditch. You climb continuously. Thick deadfall in this area makes the going tough. At 4 miles, you arrive at expansive Bailey Meadows, which interestingly, contain a small, flammable gas seep. Game trails as well as grizzly scat are everywhere. You now enter the Huck Fire Complex. The trail cuts diagonally across the north end of Bailey Meadows before crossing Bailey Creek (usually a short jump). The creek is entrenched deeply into a tiny slot in the meadow sod, about 6 feet down.

Kitten Ridge looms above the east side of the meadows. It is a steep, but beautiful, cross-country hike to its top. Elk are numerous and you get a premier view of the Tetons. From where you enter Bailey Meadows, you can see an old outfitter trail climbing Kitten Ridge directly across from where you are standing. This route ascends the spine of the ridge. Carry plenty of treated water from Bailey Creek and start early in the morning on hot summer days. Once you reach the top, the view of the Tetons and Jackson Lake is remarkable. Massive Big Game Ridge looms to the north. To the south lie the great sedimentary peaks of the Gros Ventre Range, Snow King Mountain and Jackson Hole, Mount Leidy, and the snowcapped Wind River Range.

Walk the spine of Kitten Ridge to Kitten/9160 on your topo at 8 miles. At times, there will be a trail and at times there won't. The Huck Fire had only a marginal effect on the canopy of Kitten Ridge. You can see the scale of this giant fire complex beneath you, extending virtually as far as the eye can see. From here, head due west on the ridge, through a conifer thicket. The ridge then bends back to the left, and you continue to walk the spine. Now you start to lose elevation rapidly. That hill you see above the canyon of West Pilgrim is point x8724 on your Two Ocean Lake quad. Once you're due east of it, head down a grassy hill to the drainage between you and point x8724. Head due east over the top and arrive at some beautiful meadows with blue spruce, Engelmann spruce, and Douglas-fir. The views from here are spectacular. You are 5.5 miles from Bailey Meadows and 9.5 miles from the trailhead.

Head due east, descending steadily, but not too steeply. Eventually, you'll cliff out above West Pilgrim Creek. Walk southeast now, along the cliffs. The going is tough. Soon you arrive at a giant landslide. Pick your way around it by going directly above it, and just beyond, go around a smaller landslide. From here, you'll see the way down through the lodgepole pine. Descend steeply, eventually arriving at the bottom at 11.5 miles without too much trouble. By late summer, West Pilgrim Creek is dry. The Two Ocean Lake quad erroneously shows a trail in this drainage, as does the Bridger-Teton National Forest map. We found evidence that a trail probably existed here many years ago but is all but gone now.

Head south down the little valley to Pilgrim Creek Trail, which you reach in 0.5 mile. The canyon of Pilgrim Creek is broad here and chock-full of gravel from flooding. Turn left (northeast) and head upstream. Pilgrim Creek is a large and wild valley. It is as fine a place to escape people as you'll find in Wyoming. Moose are common sights in the meadows in their constant search for willows. Pilgrim Creek has its grizzly bears, too. You can sense them in the long shadows of the evening. If you stand right next to Pilgrim Creek, you get a sublime view of the Tetons downstream. This is how Colter saw them the first time: in a wild place—not from some roadside turnout.

The trail reenters the forest and soon crosses a stream with a deep mud bottom. Before long, you cross Wildcat Creek just above its junction with Pilgrim Creek. The Tetons are partially visible from the trail now, their sharp crests rising above the gentle, forested ridges that line Pilgrim Creek.

A short distance past Wildcat Creek, you reach the signed junction with the East Rodent Trail at 12.3 miles. It enters a dense stand of lodgepole pine to your left. On this trail you climb steadily out of the Pilgrim Creek valley and in 0.5 mile come to a small clearing where the burn begins. Over the next mile, you pass through an interesting burn mosaic that is predominantly lodgepole pine. At 13.8 miles, enter an area of total burn where the trail becomes faint and is often covered with deadfall. At 14.3 miles, the trail disappears in a burned meadow that grows a bumper crop of cow parsnip in July and August. In season lupine, low larkspur, Indian paintbrush, trumpet flower, and grandfather's whiskers wash the landscape with a mosaic of color that defies description. The trail climbs halfway up the side of a small bench to your left (west-northwest). This area is often frequented by grizzly bears. We chased several off their day beds throughout this stretch and saw much evidence of feeding activity.

At 15.3 miles, you arrive at a meadow with a fine view of the Tetons, Gros Ventre Range, and Mount Leidy. Continue climbing and leave the burn at 15.8 miles. At 16.3 miles, reach Wildcat Ridge at a saddle. An old signpost (no sign) stands in the middle of the saddle; to your left (west) is the trail to Wildcat Peak with its sweeping views and to your right (east) is the trail

Brown's grave at Brown Meadows. RALPH MAUGHAN PHOTO

along Wildcat Ridge that leads to the junction with Pilgrim Creek Trail and Whetstone and West Whetstone Trails. These trails are for the wilderness savvy only. From here, you descend into the watershed of East Rodent Creek. The trail is vague, uncut, overgrown, and loaded with deadfall. But it is surprisingly easy to follow.

At 16.8 miles, cross East Rodent Creek on rocks and, at 18.8 miles cross the side stream that is west of point 7947T on your Huckleberry Mountain quad. At 19 miles, ford East Rodent again (difficult, if not dangerous, in high water). The trail climbs to a small bench on the east side of the creek. Be careful on this stretch, as the footway is eroding due to lack of use.

At 19.2 miles, the trail disappears in a meadow near a small outfitter camp. Stay in the center of the meadow and the trail will reappear faint and begin to descend steadily. At 20 miles, you reach the ford of Rodent Creek. Rodent Creek Trail is on the other side (no sign). Turn left (west) and head upstream. Another mile brings you to a meadow where the trail forks at the margin of the Huck Fire Complex. Take the left fork and enter the burn. The canyon tightens and you quickly rise 100 feet above the creek on a trail that climbs steadily. At 22 miles, arrive at Brown Meadows and the junction with the Arizona Creek and Huckleberry Ridge Trails. Before the three-way junction, you pass a grave with a wooden cross bearing the weathered inscription "T. Brown 1881." Little is known about Brown, but I sensed his soul was at rest as I sat by his grave late one afternoon and watched elk cautiously emerge from the forest to graze on his peaceful meadow. As night descended, the increasing numbers of dark shapes made tranquility fade, and I retreated to the warmth of the fire at my camp. Brown Meadows gets more than its share of grizzly bears.

From the unsigned three-way junction, head southwest across the southernmost flank of Huckleberry Ridge, well above Arizona Creek, which is far below in its canyon. Descend steeply for 1 mile until you reach the floor of the canyon with the creek roaring to your left. At 23.5 miles, ford Arizona Creek, which is swift, although not particularly deep. Another 2 miles brings you back to Bailey Meadows, where you can retrace your steps back to the trailhead.

Options: Turn right at the fork in the Rodent Creek Trail at 21 miles, on an outfitter trail that goes directly to the Huckleberry Ridge Trail and lookout. From here, head south to Brown Meadows and the junction with Arizona Creek Trail. This adds 4 miles to the loop.

3 Big Game Ridge Loop

See Map on Page 34

Highlights: An extended trip through some of the most remote and least-traveled backcountry in the contiguous 48 states. A good look at the effects of and recovery from the 1988 fires. The views from Big Game Ridge are among the finest in the American West.

Type of trip: Backpacking loop.

Total distance: 60.6 miles.

Difficulty: Strenuous.

Maps: USGS Two Ocean Lake, Huckleberry Mountain, Bobcat Ridge, Gravel Peak, Crooked Creek, and Mount Hancock quads. Bridger-Teton National Forest map, Buffalo and Jackson Ranger Districts.

Finding the trailhead: Drive north of Moran Junction 7.5 miles on U.S. Highway 89/191/287 and turn right on Pilgrim Creek Road. Follow this good dirt road 2 miles to the trailhead and park. The Pilgrim Creek Trail begins at the tiny fence line behind the parking area.

Parking and trailhead facilities: This trailhead is in Grand Teton National Park. Teton Wilderness users can park overnight, no camping.

Key points:

3.0	Great meadows.
5.5	Wide bottom of Pilgrim Creek Canyon.
12.7	Four-way junction at a saddle (8765 on Bobcat Ridge quad).
15.7	Unsigned Middle Trail junction.
20.7	Y intersection at Wolverine Creek and Gravel Creek Trails.
28.0	Fox Park.
29.0	Yellowstone National Park boundary. South Boundary Trail junction.
34.0	Top of Big Game Ridge.
43.0	Leave South Boundary Trail headed west-southwest.
43.5	Teton Wilderness boundary.
48.6	Junction with East Rodent–Middle Pilgrim Trail.
51.6	Wildcat Ridge.
54.6	Junction with Pilgrim Creek Trail.

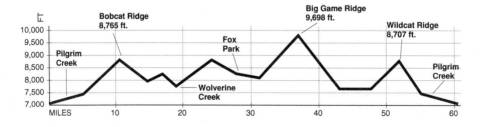

The hike: This long, remote journey is one of the finest in the American West and a wilderness experience that will provide you with a lifetime of memories. When you're back in the work world, your mind will often wander to the special places you visited here in the magnificent Teton Wilderness. Just describing this hike to you makes us crave another journey into this incredible landscape as soon as the snow lifts its veil and the flowers bloom. Enough of the accolades, let's go on an epic trip.

This loop involves innumerable fords. Have a good pair of sandals and keep them handy. Skill with a compass is an absolute must here, as many of the trails are faint and difficult to follow. However, if you pay close attention to the directions laid out in the following pages, you will have no difficulty. The first 5 miles of the hike also contain copious amounts of large deadfall, so allocate adequate time to negotiate this section.

First, put on your sandals and tie your boots to your pack because you are about to become intimately familiar with Pilgrim Creek. Ford the creek at 0.1 mile and continue upstream. Pilgrim Creek Canyon is dead ahead. At 0.3 mile, pass the park boundary and enter the Bridger...Teton National Forest. At 0.4 mile, the trail disappears. Ford the creek and the trail reappears in the willows on the north side. Immediately, the frenzy of the South Entrance Road fades away as primeval wilderness envelops you. The deadfall will slow your progress from here on, so be patient and try to find the path of least resistance. Frustration can lead to falls that result in injury, and anyone who has been impaled by a sharp branch of a fallen conifer knows what we are talking about. There is no hurrying through here, so take your time. The trail becomes faint and little used, and blowouts are common.

At 1 mile, arrive at the wilderness boundary and ford of Pilgrim Creek. As soon as you emerge from the water, notice the giant subalpine fir. This tree was here long before Colter gazed on the Tetons.

At 1.2 miles, arrive at a blowout. Go around to the right. Here the trail disappears entirely in a second and much larger landslide. The opposite bank is thick with willows, so the best way to find the trail is to walk upstream in Pilgrim Creek. As soon as you see standing trees on the south side, leave the creek and find the faint trail. Luckily, someone came through and ax-blazed this section, or it would be a very strenuous bushwhack. Follow these blazes as best you can.

Over the next mile, the trail fords Pilgrim Creek seven times, and at 2.5 miles, you can put your boots back on. The trail climbs for 0.5 mile before dropping into a large and beautiful meadow. Wildflowers are prolific in July and August. Stop here and eat lunch and rest from your toil. Also, put on your sandals, because you will ford again at 3.5 miles. At 3.7 miles, ford again and plunge into thick willows. This is an excellent place to spot moose. The willows end and the trail reappears, still in the huge meadow. At 4.4 miles, arrive at a large area of quicksand that is best passed to the right. We saw many large grizzly tracks here.

At 4.5 miles, arrive at the next ford. The meadow continues, a sea of grass and wildflowers. At 5.2 miles, arrive at the old West Pilgrim Trail, which disappears quickly in the burn. Shortly after, at 5.5 miles, you arrive at the widest part of the valley near a sandy beach next to Pilgrim Creek. The trail reenters the forest and soon crosses a stream with a deep mud bottom. Before long, you cross Wildcat Creek just above its junction with Pilgrim Creek. The Tetons are slightly visible above the gentle, forested ridges that line Pilgrim Creek.

At 6 miles, you reach the junction with the East Rodent–Middle Pilgrim Trail, which is your return route. At 7.2 miles, the trail fords. From here it negotiates the much tighter canyon of Pilgrim Creek as it ascends Bobcat Ridge. You will cross the creek continuously. The trail climbs steeply and fords five times in the next mile. At 8.2 miles, arrive at a meadow with good views of the Tetons and Bobcat Ridge. The trail continues climbing, with two more stream crossings. At 11 miles, the trail arrives at a high meadow with an outfitter camp, which is often dirty and littered. The trail now turns left and heads north, climbing steeply. At 11.2 miles, the trail forks. Bear right and climb northeast through the burn. Pilgrim Creek is just a small stream in a little canyon to your right. Although this is a tough climb on a faint trail with thick deadfall, you won't have any problems following it. When you need to catch your breath, turn around and enjoy the good view of the Tetons. At 12.2 miles, arrive at a sign that says, "Wildcat Ridge, Coulter Creek Trail." Go straight on the faint, but discernible, trail. Cross a small stream and at 12.7 miles, arrive at a saddle—8765 on the Bobcat Ridge quad—with a pond and a faint, unsigned junction with four trails, including the West Whetstone Trail, Whetstone Creek Trail, Wildcat Ridge Trail (very faint), as well as the trail you just hiked.

Remote Coulter Creek in the Teton Wilderness. RALPH MAUGHAN PHOTO

If you have some time and want a spectacular view, look northeast from where you're standing toward a high, treeless ridge (marked as 9187 on your Bobcat Ridge quad). Climb it and take in a panorama that includes the Tetons, Jackson Lake, all of the huge Pilgrim Creek drainage, the distant Gros Ventre Range, Big Game Ridge, Two Ocean Plateau, and far-distant Younts Peak on the Continental Divide near the border of the Washakie Wilderness.

Back on the main trail, go straight east from the pond on the faint Whetstone Creek Trail. Now you start a long, gentle, 765-foot descent toward Coulter Creek through a beautiful and largely unburned mosaic of lodgepole pine, subalpine fir, and whitebark pine. The trail follows a contour above an unnamed tributary of Coulter Creek. At 14.2 miles, the trail disappears in a large meadow near Coulter Creek. You'll see a signless post as you ramble toward Coulter Creek. You will also notice that Coulter Creek is entirely burned. From the meadow, head downstream 0.1 mile to a ford. Coulter Creek is quite a torrent early in the summer and is never crossed with dry feet, even in late August. You can cross it here the same way the grizzly bears do, on a big log bridging the creek. It is easy. We saw pan-sized bear scats on both sides of the log. Now head north along Coulter Creek and back into the 1988 burn. The trail is faint again, with heavy deadfall. You can avoid the many fords on this segment by simply climbing around them. Pass a medium-sized gorge on your left and pick your way down Coulter Creek. At 15.7 miles, leave the burn and arrive at the ruins of an old cabin. Only the foundation remains. A large side stream flowing into Coulter Creek on the right just beyond the ruins can be a little confusing because it is about the same size as Coulter Creek. The unsigned Middle Trail begins amidst the gravel on the south side of this stream. This is an extremely enjoyable and beautiful trail, especially the Coulter Creek side. Surprisingly, it is in reasonable condition when you consider its very remote location. The trail takes you through three superlative meadows over 3 miles on its way to Wolverine Creek. Once you reach the bottom of the Wolverine Creek valley, the trail disappears in a bog. There is much quicksand in this area, so head for higher ground and walk around the bog.

At 18.7 miles, you arrive at the ford of Wolverine Creek. Once you're across, pick up the track in a great meadow and arrive at the junction with the Wolverine Creek Trail. You might see the remnants of an old sign at the edge of these meadows. The maps show a trail headed down Wolverine Creek to its confluence with Coulter Creek. This trail does not exist. All you'll find are bogs and quicksand. Of course, solitude and adventure are guaranteed to those who seek out this remote country.

Now turn right (east) and immediately enter a giant, unsightly, and permanent outfitter camp. At 19.7 miles, pass a pond on your right and then descend to a ford of an unnamed tributary that plunges steeply off the face of Big Game Ridge in a narrow canyon. At 20.7 miles, the trail arrives at a junction where Wolverine Creek Trail and Gravel Creek Trail intersect. Bear left on the faint outfitter trail and continue upstream. Over the next 4 miles, this trail is sometimes hard to follow. I've never seen more grizzly sign anywhere in the contiguous 48 states than on this section of trail.

Now reenter the burn and start climbing. The trail quickly becomes a faint, rough trace. At 21.7 miles, cross tiny Wolverine Creek in a small gorge where it pours off massive Big Game Ridge. As you climb steeply into this remote part of the Pinyon Peak Highlands, you get good views of Pinyon Peak, Coulter Creek and Rodent Creek drainages, Kitten Ridge and, in the distance, Mount Moran. At 22.2 miles, the trail turns left (north) on a tree-less side ridge and really starts to climb. The trail disappears at 22.5 miles. You are near 8649T on the Gravel Peak quad. Climb 60 degrees east-north-east across this treeless ridge and in 0.25 miles the trail reappears heading due east. Within 100 yards you cross a small stream. At 23 miles, the trail disappears again. Continue due east 50 yards and it reappears suddenly. The trail descends to a small stream valley and enters live forest with abun-dant whitebark pine, the nut of which is a prime delicacy of our ursal hosts. Strangely enough, the footway is extremely distinct for the next 0.3 mile, where it again disappears in a small meadow. Cross the meadow to the line of burned trees on its east side. Turn left and climb uphill (north) and pick the trail up again shortly. The trail is very faint now, a stark contrast to its condition in the live forest only 30 feet away. At 23.7 miles, the trail arrives at a small stream in a 25-foot-deep valley where it again disappears, only to reappear at the top of the hill above the stream. Now you climb steadily to the top of the divide between Fox Creek and Wolverine Creek, at 8833AT on your Gravel Peak quad.

Notice the pond on your right in a small clearing. In September 1996 we noticed abundant bear sign here, including that of a sow and cub. On the high spot to your left (north) is a large stand of live whitebark pine, the reason for the thick grizzly sign. The cones were abundant and chock-full of nuts when we were there. We tasted the nuts to see what the fuss was about, but found them extremely bitter.

Just beyond the pond, the trail disappears. Bear right (south-southeast) and locate a second, smaller pond. The trail bears southeast, circles the right side of this pond, and starts to descend noticeably, disappearing on the way downhill. No matter, the Big Game Ridge cutoff is in sight. This area is unburned, and whitebark pine is everywhere. The cutoff is in a meadow that is a spectacular scene of wavy grass, wildflowers, bees, and humming-birds. The late summer display is superb, with yellow paintbrush dominat-ing the scene. At 24.7 miles, arrive at a highly weathered sign that simply says "Big Game Ridge." Bear left (north) and begin the gradual descent to Fox Park. You are truly in the back of beyond. As you descend, the views of Two Ocean Plateau, Big Game Ridge, and the Red Hills in Yellowstone Na-tional Park are sublime. At 26 miles, arrive at the junction with the Mink Creek Cutoff Trail. The sign was on the ground in 1996. Now you begin to descend in earnest toward Fox Park. At 26.7 miles, reach the first of the meadows. This is superb wildlife habitat that epitomizes what I think of when I conjure up the image of the Yellowstone ecosystem. Fox Creek tumbles through this big, wild, and beautiful meadow. At 27 miles, reach a

The Snake River at Fox Park. RALPH MAUGHAN PHOTO

Y intersection in the meadow. The right fork is marked with a small sign that says "trail." Just beyond that you ford Fox Creek. At 27.5 miles, arrive at the signed junction with the Snake River Trail, which says "Yellowstone 1." Bear left. At 28 miles, you come to the ford of the Snake River. The great expanse of Fox Park unfolds before you. The mighty Snake River flows through here near its seldom-visited headwaters. Now you enter live forest with the Snake River to your left in a rapidly deepening canyon. At 28.5 miles, arrive at an unsigned junction where you take a sharp left and follow the river. The trail bears north-northwest and climbs around the canyon 0.25 mile. At 29 miles, arrive at the Yellowstone National Park boundary and the South Boundary Trail junction. Fox Park Patrol Cabin is directly ahead. A sign here says, "Snake River 0.5; Harebell Cabin 12."

Most of the South Boundary Trail is in Yellowstone National Park, and we will not describe it in the scope of our guide. However, the portion over Big Game Ridge wanders in and out of the Teton Wilderness. If you camp along this stretch of the hike, make sure you are in the Teton Wilderness and not the park. The boundary is well marked. In dry years, there is no water along Big Game Ridge. Plan accordingly.

Within 0.5 mile of the cabin, arrive at a sign that says "Snake River." The first crossing is a small side channel; the real ford is 0.1 mile ahead. A tenth of a mile after the fords, arrive at the junction where the Snake River Trail cuts off and follows the river. Go straight (west) at a sign that says "Harebell Cabin via South Boundary Trail 11.5." Now begin a grueling 4-mile climb to the top of Big Game Ridge, which you reach at 34 miles.

The trail rambles at timberline for about 3 miles before crossing at a high point on the ridge at 9,900 feet for a 360-degree view. As you cross the ridge, look northward into Yellowstone across a deep, unnamed canyon through which the Snake River flows. Beyond that you see Heart Lake and Yellowstone Lake (through your binoculars you should be able to see the Lake Lodge on the north end of the lake). Still farther lies the forested Mirror Plateau, the north boundary of Yellowstone and the Absaroka and Gallatin Ranges in Montana. To the east (from left to right) stretches the craggy outline of the Absaroka Mountains, more than 100 miles in length. Southward your view soars over the Pinyon Peak Highlands and flies farther to the Mount Leidy Highlands, finally resting on the wild peaks of the Gros Ventre Range. Far to the south you can see the Snake River Range and to the distant southeast, a bit of the mighty Wind River Range. To the west, the Tetons scrape the sky and shine in the midday sun. Just north of them you can make out the Henry's Lake Mountains on the Idaho-Montana border, while in the fore-ground is the forested Pitchstone Plateau of Yellowstone. Few places in the American West command such a view.

At 37 miles, enter the burn and start a steep descent. At 38 miles, switchbacks, though steep, help ease the trip down. At 40 miles, Harebell Creek appears on your left, just before you cross it. There is no water in dry years. The trail leaves the creek in a deep gorge. Now a knee-buckling descent begins until you rejoin Harebell Creek at 41 miles. At 41.5 miles, reach Harebell Cabin and another junction with the Snake River Trail. Stay on the South Boundary Trail and head west at a sign that says "South Entrance 12." Leave the burn and enter a thick lodgepole pine forest. Continue for 1.5 miles on the up-and-down trail toward Coulter Creek. Once the canyon widens, head south-southwest off the trail. About half a mile from the trail, you arrive at the Teton Wilderness boundary. Continue until you reach Wolverine Creek, 1 mile from where you left the South Boundary Trail. Find a suitable place to ford (it is deep and swift) and pick up the Coulter Creek Trail through the willows on the west side of the creek. Watch out for quicksand through here. At 44.4 miles, the trail comes to the confluence of Coulter Creek and Wolverine Creek. A sign says "Trail" and a path leads to a ford of Coulter Creek. Ignore them because this trail disappears just beyond the outfitter camp on the other side. Contrary to what maps show, there is no trail along this section of Wolverine Creek. Instead, turn right (south), find the trail on the other side of the deadfall, and head up Coulter Creek. This section of the trail is quite beautiful and climbs relentlessly above the gorge of Coulter Creek through dense, live forest. At 47 miles, it turns right again at a much smaller stream. This stream is Rodent Creek, and the trail is now the Rodent Creek Trail.

The trail stays above the creek for 1 mile and then descends to the creek, where it begins a series of seven fords over the next 0.5 mile through a narrow gorge. After the seventh ford, the valley widens. Keep your eyes peeled on the south side of Rodent Creek. Shortly beyond the last ford, at 48.6 miles, East Rodent–Creek tumbles into Rodent Creek. Ford Rodent just above East Rodent and find the East Rodent–Middle Pilgrim Trail on the west side of East Rodent Creek. It is easy to find once you've located the mouth of East Rodent Creek.

Refer to Kitten Ridge Loop (Hike 2) for the description (in reverse) of the next 6 miles back to Pilgrim Creek Trail. From there, you reverse the first 6 miles of the Big Game Ridge Loop back to the trailhead.

4 Whetstone Loop

See Map on Page 34

Highlights:	A rigorous wilderness loop through some of the most remote country in the contiguous 48 states; numerous meadows, ponds, and wildlife.
Type of hike:	Backpacking loop.
Total distance:	22.5 miles.
Difficult:	Moderate.
Maps:	USGS Bobcat Ridge and Whetstone Mountain quads; Bridger-Teton National Forest map, Buffalo and Jackson Ranger Districts.

Finding the trailhead: From Moran Junction, drive north on U.S. Highway 89/191/287 for 1.2 miles to the paved Pacific Creek Road and turn right at the sign. Pass the road to Two Ocean Lake at 1.5 miles and just beyond, come to another junction. Take the unpaved fork to the left. A sign tells you this is the road to the Teton Wilderness. From here it is 5 miles to Pacific Creek Campground and the trailhead, which is exactly at the edge of the wilderness.

Parking and trailhead facilities: Pacific Creek Campground (fee) has adequate camping, abundant parking, outhouses, picnic tables, bear-proof refuse containers, and potable water.

Key points:
1.5	Junction with Whetstone Creek–West Cutoff Trail.
4.5	Unsigned junction with East Whetstone Creek Trail.
6.0	Meadow on East Whetstone.
9.2	Saddle between East Whetstone and Coulter Creek.
11.0	Meadows on Coulter Creek.
13.5	Unsigned junction with Whetstone Creek Trail.
15.0	Four-way junction at the saddle at 8765 on your Bobcat Ridge quad.

The hike: This country is the place to be during an election year. It is extremely wild and, except during hunting season, receives little or no use. It provides excellent opportunities for viewing wildlife as well as ghostly apparitions in the form of burned trees. The hike goes through an area that experiences heavy ongoing landslides, which increases the challenge presented by this loop. Contact the Bridger-Teton National Forest for updated conditions.

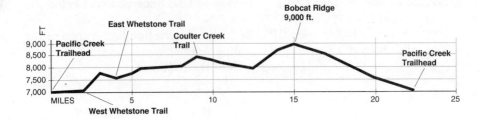

You start from one of the busiest trailheads in the wilderness. Once you leave the friendly cottonwoods, you enter a diverse forest. Besides lodge-pole pine, you'll observe Engelmann spruce, some Douglas-fir, with a few aspens, too. The broad trail climbs gradually, affording some nice views of Pacific Creek if you seek them out. At 1.5 miles, you arrive at the junction with Whetstone Creek–West Cutoff Trail, marked by a wooden sign nailed to a tree. The trail ascends on gentle switchbacks for an 800-foot climb over the shoulder of Whetstone Mountain. You'll pass through a beautiful forest of pine, spruce, and fir, in which nestle many ponds. Finally descend to a large and beautiful meadow at the confluence of West Whetstone and East Whetstone Creeks, 4.5 miles from the trailhead. Ford West Whetstone Creek just above the confluence. There was no sign for the East Whetstone Creek Trail in 1997. Perhaps one will have been erected when you get here. There is no trail for the first mile, due to massive landslide activity in the narrow canyon of East Whetstone Creek. Put on your sandals and slosh upstream. It is not difficult because the creek is usually quite shallow by mid-July. The creek is surrounded by willows. We saw a sow grizzly and her cub here feeding in July 1997. One mile above the confluence, the trail appears on the left side of the stream. It has been recut and is easy to follow. It climbs gradually to a saddle between East Whetstone and Coulter Creeks.

At 6 miles, the trail crosses the creek and enters a huge and beautiful meadow, and at 7.2 miles, crosses back at an outfitter camp. You reach the saddle between East Whetstone and Coulter Creeks at 9.2 miles and start your descent into the beautiful and remote headwaters of Coulter Creek on the Coulter Creek Trail. The forest is entirely burned. At 10 miles, you reach the crossing of tiny Coulter Creek, flowing from its source at the base of 9,704-foot-high Pinyon Peak. Find this point east of 8353T on your Bobcat Ridge quad. For a scenic diversion, follow Coulter Creek up to the meadows where it bubbles out of the ground, about 1 mile from the trail. From here, climb steeply to the summit of Pinyon Peak. The Tetons tower to the west. Mount Leidy and the Gros Ventre Range are to the south, while the Teton Wilderness unfolds to the east. Big Game Ridge dominates the north sky-line, always looking inviting. To continue the hike, return to Coulter Creek Trail the same way you came.

From the first crossing of Coulter Creek, the trail descends steadily to a huge expanse of meadows that you reach at 11 miles. As you can see on your Bobcat Ridge quad, the trail circles around this sea of grass, staying in

48

the burned forest at its edge. It disappears frequently, but is always easily found again. In wet years, it is rather boggy. The canyon tightens immediately at the end of the meadow, and the trail fords now-much-larger Coulter Creek. You climb to a bench in burned forest well above the canyon of Coulter Creek. The trail is easy to follow for about 1 mile, then it vanishes abruptly. You are within 0.5 mile of the junction with Whetstone Creek Trail. Head downstream through live forest, avoiding the boggy areas as best you can until you arrive at a set of meadows along Coulter Creek with a signless post in the middle, which you reach at 13.5 miles. Look south from the post to a clump of conifers near one of the side streams in this drainage. If you have binoculars, you'll see a blaze on the largest of these trees. This is the humble beginning of the Whetstone Creek Trail. From the tree, head right (west) up the side canyon. About half a mile from the blaze, the trail forks. Take the right fork and climb 765 feet through a beautiful, unburned mosaic of lodgepole pine, subalpine fir, and whitebark pine. At 15 miles, arrive at a saddle with a four-way trail junction (8765 on your Bobcat Ridge quad). There is a pond here.

Want a spectacular view? Look northwest from where you're standing and see a high, treeless ridge (9187 on your Bobcat Ridge quad). Climb it and take in a panorama that includes the Tetons, Jackson Lake, all the Pilgrim Creek country, the Gros Ventre Range, Big Game Ridge, Two Ocean Plateau, and Younts Peak on the Continental Divide near the border of the Washakie Wilderness.

From the pond, head southeast through a stand lodgepole pine on an esker, and the West Whetstone Trail will materialize and take you down through a meadow where it abruptly disappears in an area of deadfall. Look a little southeast to the left of Bobcat Ridge itself. The notch you see is where you're headed. Now set the controls for 146 degrees east and bust

Whetstone Mountain from Pacific Creek. RALPH MAUGHAN PHOTO

Tetons from Pacific Creek Meadows. RALPH MAUGHAN PHOTO

through a nasty deadfall. In less than 100 yards, you'll pick up the trail again. It is faint in spots and chock-full of deadfall (the deadfall goes all the way back to Pacific Creek, so plan on this section taking more time), but the prize is the notch, and if you focus on that, you won't lose the trail. After the notch, the trail descends a giant switchback to the valley of West Whetstone Creek. From here, except for the frequently encountered deadfall, the trail is easy to follow.

The valley of West Whetstone Creek is mostly burned with numerous small landslides. After 4 miles, you'll reach a series of three fords, all of which are easy. After the third ford, arrive at the meadow and the confluence of East Whetstone and West Whetstone Creeks. Retrace your steps 3.5 miles back to the trailhead.

5 Lava Creek

Highlights: A little-used trail to a scenic and remote valley.
Type of hike: Out-and-back base camp or day hike.
Total distance: 16 miles (or less).
Difficulty: Easy.
Maps: USGS Davis Hill, Whetstone Mountain, and Gravel Mountain quads; Bridger-Teton National Forest map, Buffalo and Jackson Ranger Districts.

Finding the trailhead: From Moran Junction, head east 3 miles on U.S. Highway 26/287 to Buffalo Valley Road. Turn left and drive 3 miles down this road to the trailhead on the left. It is little used—just a grassy spot immediately next to Buffalo Valley Road. The trailhead is near an aspen grove, but there is no shade. The trailhead has a Forest Service information sign, but no sign indicating that it is the Lava Creek Trailhead.

Parking and trailhead facilities: Unimproved.

Key points:
2.8 Unnamed "pass" between Buffalo River and Lava Creek drainages.
5.2 Ford of Lava Creek.

The hike: If you're day hiking this one, just walk in as far as you choose, and return the same way. The trail is faint, but it becomes much more evident as you climb, crossing an open slope with patches of small aspens and many wildflowers (at least until mid- to late July). There are good views of Buffalo Valley to the south and the Mount Leidy Highlands south of that.

Eventually the slope becomes an open forest with some very big Douglas-fir. This is a mixed forest of not just Douglas-fir, but subalpine fir, lodgepole pine, Englemann spruce, and quaking aspen. You pass lots of small meadows until you reach the top where the trail crosses over the west shoulder of Mount Randolph. The trail climbs to the pass almost continuously, although sometimes the climb is gentle and at others, fairly steep. On the way to the pass are panoramic views if you bother to walk 100 yards or so off the trail to seek them out. At 2.8 miles, reach the pass and begin a gentle descent to Lava Creek. The drop into the canyon of Lava Creek generally follows down-sloping benches on the moist backside of Mount Randolph. These benches are broken by a number of steeper descents. The backside is

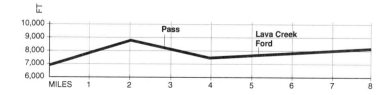

Lava Creek • Enos Lake Loop
Holmes Cave • Buffalo Forks Loop

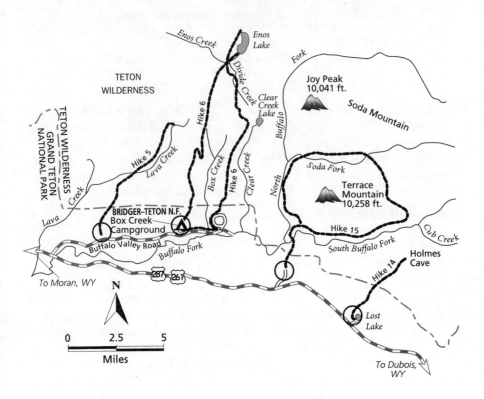

heavily forested. As a result you get only glimpses of the odd profile of Gravel Mountain that rises to the north and northwest of Lava Creek. A couple of rivulets on the backside run most of the summer and can be used as water sources. At 5.2 miles, arrive at the ford of Lava Creek. It is an easy crossing after snowmelt is complete.

Once you cross the stream, weird Gravel Mountain, with its steep, sedimentary conglomerate slopes, dominates the landscape. The trail goes through extensive and beautiful meadows up Lava Creek. At 8 miles, the trail begins climbing away from Lava Creek and crosses through the wreckage wrought by the Teton Tornado (August 1987). Your hike ends here. Backtrack to the Lava Creek Trailhead.

On the shoulder of Mt. Randolph, Lava Creek Trail. RALPH MAUGHAN PHOTO

6 Enos Lake Loop

See Map on Page 52

Highlights:	The earliest access (mid-June most years) deep into the Teton Wilderness; wildlife; Enos Lake.
Type of hike:	Backpacking loop.
Total distance:	20 miles.
Difficulty:	Moderate.
Maps:	USGS Rosies Ridge, Gravel Mountain, Joy Peak, and Angle Mountain quads; Bridger-Teton National Forest map, Buffalo and Jackson Ranger Districts.

Finding the trailhead: From Moran Junction, head east 3 miles on Highway 26/287 to Buffalo Valley Road. Turn left and drive 8 miles to the signed junction with the gravel road to Box Creek Trailhead. Turn left (north). The road leads a short distance uphill to Box Creek Campground (fee).

Parking and trailhead facilities: There are six campsites, outhouses, picnic tables, a signboard, ample parking, and stock-watering troughs. There is no potable water.

Key points:

- 4.0   Meadow at the base of Gravel Ridge.
- 10.0   Enos Lake.
- 16.0   Clear Creek Meadows.
- 18.5   Turpin Meadows.

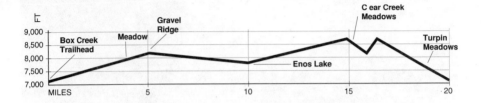

The hike: This is a near loop that requires 1.5 miles of road walking between the Box Creek and Clear Creek Trailheads. You can go all the way to Enos Lake by mid-June most years. In late summer, flowing water may be scarce. During the June snowmelt you have to cross snowmelt streams, but none of the fords are difficult. Much of the hike goes through the weird remains of the Teton Tornado, a most unusual pile of forest rubble from the great wind event of 1987.

The Box Creek Trail climbs diagonally up the side hill through a meadow with a good view of the Mount Leidy country across the Buffalo Valley to the south. Soon thereafter, the trail enters the forest and views disappear. The wilderness boundary is reached at 0.5 mile, and the trail continues its gradual climb. You reach a low pass at 2 miles and drop gradually for the next 2 miles to a meadow at the base of Gravel Ridge. The trail then makes a 180-degree turn around the meadow and abruptly begins its ascent of Gravel Ridge. You gain views of the leading edge of the Teton Tornado lumber pile and unusual-shaped Gravel Mountain to the west and northwest as you ascend Gravel Ridge. A climb of 300 feet in 0.5 mile brings you to the top of the ridge, which is open, with scattered conifers and fine views of the Teton Tornado rubble and the high plateaus off to the east. You descend Gravel Ridge, following the trail in a generally north-by-northeast direction through a series of meadows through which a headwater tributary of Box Creek runs.

Soon you enter the tornado's jack-strawed timber through which the trail was laboriously recut over a period of years. The trail crosses a low saddle to begin its descent to Enos Creek, and soon a few clearings appear among the piles of wind-thrown timber. As you descend, the remnants of the 1988 burn begin to appear on the right (east). There is no apparent regeneration of the burned fir forest. At 9 miles, you arrive at the crossing of Enos Creek. When you climb up its bank on the other side, you emerge into meadows that continue all the way to Enos Lake, which you reach at 10 miles. The lake's vicinity is rich with wildlife, especially moose, and in the early summer, elk, bear, and coyotes are common. A wolf pack used the area around the lake in the summer of 1998. Eagles and ospreys nest near the lake. I saw common loons and a pair of trumpeter swans on the lake in 1996. Numerous beavers live in holes in the moist shoreline. Sandhill cranes are also numerous. Their cries give an auditory definition to the wilderness experience in the Yellowstone ecosystem.

From the lake, return to Enos Creek and at the ford, follow the trail that goes up the middle of the three creeks. One or more may be dry in late summer. Also, the location of the trail on the Gravel Mountain quad is not correct. You climb steeply up a shallow canyon to a crossing. Here the trail leaves the creek and climbs onto a long meadow that has the tornado rubble on its west side and the burned timber from the fire on its east side. The meadow ends at a low pass at 12.8 miles. If you look backward down the meadow, you get a fine view of Gravel Peak in the distance. At the pass you drop steeply, but briefly, down into the east fork of Box Creek's headwaters, which run through a long meadow. You leave the Teton Tornado behind, but not the burn. The east slope of the meadow is burned, but the west slope is not. At the south end of the meadow (beyond which the creek soon drops into a canyon), the trail turns and climbs sharply uphill. Soon you gain your first view of the distant Tetons. You continue to climb, entering meadowy country and turning to the south. You reach a pass at 14.8 miles after gaining about 450 feet in elevation. Here you are on the edge of the Clear Creek drainage, and you can follow the small stream about half a mile to its source, pretty Clear Creek Lake. The trail never really drops into Clear Creek. Instead it stays near the ridgeline, providing good views and heading south, passing just to the east of point 8684 on the Joy Peak quad. The trail de-

Headwater meadows of Box Creek. RALPH MAUGHAN PHOTO

Clear Creek Lake. RALPH MAUGHAN PHOTO

scends and swings to the southwest around this point, and there are great vistas of the Tetons, Mount Randolph (to their left), and Gravel Mountain (to their right). From this point the trail descends through meadow, lodgepole pine and spruce-fir forest. You pass by "signed" lower route trail to Enos Lake, then continue to descend. Finally, at 16 miles, you come to expansive Clear Creek Meadows, not named on the quad. At the south end of the meadows, the trail enters the forest and descends at an increasing grade. Finally, you break out into clearings with a wonderful view of the Buffalo Valley and the Mount Leidy Highlands. Notice the craggy old-growth Douglas-fir on the lower portion just before the final, steep pitch down to the Turpin Meadows summer home area near Turpin Meadows Campground, which you reach at 18.5 miles.

Now turn right and follow Clear Creek Road 0.5 mile to Buffalo Valley Road, where you also turn right. This will take you back to the Box Creek Trailhead and your rig.

7 Two Ocean Plateau Loop

Highlights:	Parting of the Waters Natural Landmark (Continental Divide); good views, wildflowers, wildlife, and solitude.
Type of hike:	Backpacking loop.
Total distance:	44.4 miles.
Difficulty:	Moderate.
Maps:	USGS Whetstone Mountain, Gravel Mountain, Gravel Peak, and Two Ocean Pass quads; Bridger-Teton National Forest map, North Half.

Finding the trailhead: From Moran Junction, drive north on U.S. Highway 89/191/287 for 1.2 miles to the paved Pacific Creek Road and turn right at the sign. Pass the road to Two Ocean Lake at 1.5 miles and just beyond come to another junction. Take the unpaved fork to the left. A sign tells you this is the road to the Teton Wilderness. From here it is 5 miles to Pacific Creek Campground and the trailhead, which is exactly at the edge of the wilderness.

Parking and trailhead facilities: Pacific Creek Campground has adequate camping, abundant parking, outhouses, picnic tables, bear-proof containers, and potable water.

Key points:
3.9	Gravel Creek Trail junction.
4.1	Moss Lake Trail junction. (unmarked).
10.3	Mink Creek Trail junction.
17.8	Two Ocean Plateau.
18.6	Parting of the Waters Natural Landmark.
24.9	Falcon Creek Trail junction.
34.1	Pacific Creek Trail junction.

The hike: You start from one of the busiest trailheads in the wilderness. Once you leave the friendly cottonwoods, you enter a forest that is quite diverse. Besides lodgepole pine, you'll observe Engelmann spruce, some Douglas-fir, and a few aspens. The broad trail climbs gradually, affording some nice views of Pacific Creek if you seek them out.

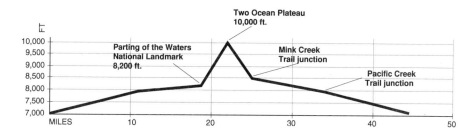

Two Ocean Plateau Loop

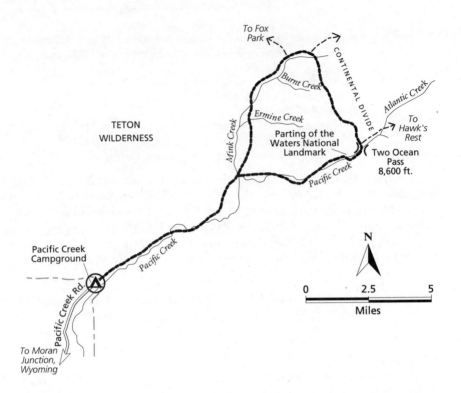

At 1.5 miles, you arrive at the junction with Whetstone Creek–West Cut-off Trail, marked by a wooden sign nailed to a tree. The ford of Whetstone Creek is at 2.1 miles and consists of multiple small channels. At 3 miles, the trail leaves the forest and enters a meadow, running in a southwest-northeast direction. Look southwest for a spectacular view of the Tetons, including Mount Moran. In July and August, wildflowers in yellows, whites, purples, and some reds splatter the green meadow with color. The effects of the burn of 1988 are visible on the north side of Pacific Creek. The meadow is open to grazing during the summer months, so use caution not to allow stock paths to lead you astray. The trail continues across the meadow for 3 miles in multiple parallel lanes and is generally in good condition. However, during the spring, early summer, or prolonged periods of heavy rain, large sections of the trail can be quite muddy.

At 3.9 miles, the Gravel Creek Trail takes off to the north. The signpost marking the trailhead has fallen and the base is surrounded by rounded cobbles and boulders. At 4.1 miles, the unmarked Moss Lake Trail takes off to the south. At 4.2 miles, you ford the one large channel of Gravel Creek. After passing over a sparsely forested terrace, the trail descends again onto the floodplain of Pacific Creek, where it winds through thick riparian brush. You pass a drying oxbow lake full of sediment and then come to the first ford of Pacific Creek at 4.5 miles. If you ford from one gravel bar to another, you can avoid the deep cutbank pools. After the ford, the trail is disguised by tall grasses and takes off almost directly in between the two meanders of the creek. The trail continues along the floodplain grasses until you ford Pacific Creek again at 5.9 miles. The trail then ascends slightly and enters a moderately dense forest untouched by the fire of 1988. You follow along the north side of Pacific Creek, winding through the forest and crossing some small tributaries that drain the south side of Gravel Peak. At 7.6 miles is the intersection of the Enos Creek Cutoff Trail, which is unmarked and difficult to find; the Pacific Creek Trail is used considerably more. After this intersection, the Pacific Creek Trail becomes moderately steep, continuing uphill for almost 2 miles. At 9.3 miles, you descend toward the confluence of Mink Creek and Pacific Creek. The descent is very muddy and deeply incised. At 10.1 miles, you arrive at the confluence. At 10.3 miles is the first turnoff to the Mink Creek Trail, at a narrow Y intersection that is easy to miss because the wooden trail sign is no longer standing.

For the next 8 miles the trail winds along Pacific Creek, alternating between high benches and meadows. Look east for a view of Two Ocean Pass in the distance. The trail travels along the outer fringe of the fire where it fingered out, leaving some areas scorched and some untouched. You can spot several beaver dams and their inhabitants along this stretch. At 11.2 miles is the second intersection of the Mink Creek Trail, marked by a wooden

Parting of the Waters at Two Ocean Pass. Atlantic Creek to the left. Pacific Creek to the right.
Ralph Maughan photo

Heading toward the Two Ocean Plateau. GWEN GERBER PHOTO

sign. You ford Pacific Creek at 11.9 miles, 14.1 miles, and then again at 16.9 miles. At 17.4 miles is the intersection with the North Buffalo Fork Trail, which is much wider and more well traveled, and the sign marking the trail intersection is still standing. Between this trail intersection and the Parting of the Waters Natural Landmark, the trail is very well maintained, with bridges over stream crossings and marshes in most areas. At 17.8 miles, following a long bridge over a marsh, a sign marks a turnoff to the right (east) to an outfitters camp. This turnoff also connects with the Atlantic Creek Trail. This is the crest of Two Ocean Plateau—the Continental Divide. A left at this trail intersection will lead to Two Ocean Trail. At 18.4 miles, the Atlantic Creek Trail intersects from the northeast, and the Pacific Creek Trail continues north to Parting of the Waters Natural Landmark at 18.6 miles. At Parting of the Waters Natural Landmark, Two Ocean Creek splits into Atlantic Creek and Pacific Creek. Atlantic Creek spills into the Atlantic Ocean after a 3,488-mile journey, while Pacific Creek enters the Pacific Ocean after a 1,353-mile journey.

Following Parting of the Waters, you begin the hike up Two Ocean Divide, a moderate climb for about 3 miles. The majority of the trees have been burned by the fire of 1988, allowing the underbrush to thrive in vivid, blooming colors. At 20 miles, you cross the east fork of Two Ocean Creek. Just downstream of the trail crossing is an angelic waterfall that pours over a moss-covered rock. The trail continues uphill to the west past a ford of the West Fork of Two Ocean Creek into a pretty cirque valley with alpine conifers and an abundance of wildflowers. As you leave the tree line and approach

Falls on the east fork of East Two Ocean Creek. GWEN GERBER PHOTO

the highest point of Two Ocean Pass, the trail curves toward the west and is marked by cairns (some with poles sticking out of the rocks). The trail leads to the highest point of the hike at 21.6 miles, and an excellent view of the Tetons and Jenny Lake at 10,078 feet. It then continues north across Two Ocean Plateau, passing by a few seasonal lakes. At 22.4 miles, you begin the 2.5-mile descent into Mink Creek valley. Looking north you can see a blowdown from the Teton Tornado. The trail is moderately steep and hard to find. After you descend into Mink Creek Valley, you enter a thick conifer forest. Once you leave the forest and enter the meadows of Mink Creek, you pass through an old campsite (a sign says "no camping"). Ford Mink Creek and travel along its north banks. Do not be led astray by a dead-end path that travels along the south side of Mink Creek. Directly after the ford of Mink Creek, at 24.9 miles, you meet the signed Falcon Creek Trail. The sign points east to Yellowstone Meadows. Continue west along Mink Creek.

At 26 miles is a signed intersection to Fox Park Patrol Cabin. This is the Mink Creek Cutoff Trail. Almost directly north of this point is the headwaters of the great Snake River. Few have traced it to its actual origin. Almost immediately after this intersection, you ford Mink Creek for the second time. The trail winds through a deep forest for more than 1 mile until it comes to an opening with a great view of an unnamed stream meandering through a valley to join Mink Creek. After a moderate descent, you ford Burnt Creek. At 30 miles, you pass an outfitter's camp set in a meadow on the east side of the trail. This is a common place for hunters to stay during the fall hunting season. Be wary of packhorse paths that may lead you astray. In the trees, directly following the outfitter's camp you reach the unsigned second intersection to the Fox Park Patrol Cabin. At 30.9 miles, you ford Ermine Creek and begin a gradual uphill climb into a conifer forest. At 32.5 miles, you begin a gradual descent back toward the intersection with Pacific Creek Trail, which you reach at 34.1 miles. Now turn left and follow Pacific Creek Trail 10.3 miles back to the trailhead.

Hike contributed by Gwen Gerber.

Continental Divide

Anyone who has studied a little geology knows that limestone, with heat, pressure, or liquid, becomes marble. Metaphorically, Hikes 8, 9, 10, and 11 can be viewed as growing out of one another. Hike 8 provides access to Hike 9, which in turn provides access to Hikes 10 and 11. Simply refer to the key points in the preceding hike to determine the point from which you start the next hike. The trailheads for Hikes 9, 10, and 11 are in the backcountry; you can provide your own heat, pressure, or liquid.

8 Upper Brooks Lake

Highlights:	An easy hike to a beautiful alpine lake near the Continental Divide.
Type of hike:	Out-and-back day hike.
Total distance:	6 miles.
Difficulty:	Easy.
Maps:	USGS Togwotee Pass quad; Bridger-Teton National Forest map, Buffalo and Jackson Ranger Districts.

Finding the trailhead: From Moran Junction, travel 30 miles east on U.S. Highway 26/287 (toward Dubois) to Forest Service 515 on your left. There is a sign indicating that it is the road to Brooks Lake. This point is 5.3 miles east of Togwotee Pass. Follow FS 515 for 5 miles to its end at the Yellowstone Trailhead, which is just beyond the campground.

Parking and trailhead facilities: Brooks Lake Campground (fee) has 14 sites, picnic tables, potable water, outhouses, and bear-proof refuse containers. There is room for several cars at the trailhead parking area.

Key points:
- 1.0 Ford of Brooks Lake Creek.
- 3.0 Upper Brooks Lake.

The hike: The signed Yellowstone Trail leaves from the parking lot and heads around the west side of Brooks Lake. The Forest Service has constructed new boardwalks, preserving wetland habitat and the waterproofing on your boots. Brooks Lake is large. The lakeside scene is dominated by

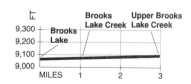

Upper Brooks Lake • Ferry Lake Loop
Jade Lakes • Bonneville Pass

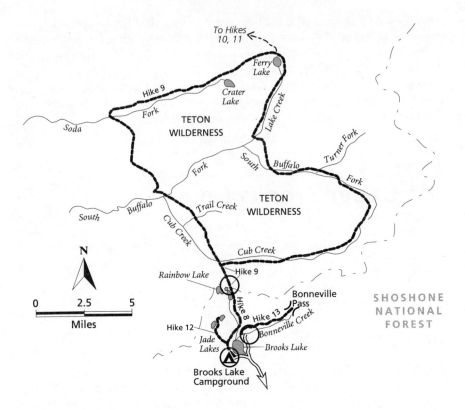

the towering, jagged battlements of Pinnacle Buttes just east of the lake. They are more than 11,000 feet in elevation. To the west rise the stunning Breccia Cliffs. Lacking the pinnacles of the mountains to the east, the Breccia Cliffs present a uniform 500- to 800-foot-high wall all the way to Upper Brooks Lake.

Once around the lake, the trail climbs about 80 feet and passes on the west side of a small, forested hill. Then the trail descends gradually to a crossing of Brooks Lake Creek at 1 mile. From here the trail is often wet as a result of the downpours that frequently occur (it has rained every time we've been to Brooks Lake), and the resulting claylike gumbo mud sticks to your boots in 5-pound clumps.

The trail keeps to the east side of the lengthy, nearly level meadow from the creek crossing to Upper Brooks Lake, which you reach at 3 miles.

Options: A trail loops around the north side of Upper Brooks Lake and climbs to scenic Rainbow Lake in another mile.

Upper Brooks Lake and the Pinnacle Buttes. RALPH MAUGHAN PHOTO

9 Ferry Lake Loop

See Map on Page 64

Highlights:	A beautiful hike through diverse habitats full of wildlife.
Type of hike:	Backpacking loop.
Total distance:	45 miles.
Difficulty:	Moderate.
Maps:	USGS Togwotee Pass, Dundee Meadows, Ferry Lake, and Crater Lakequads; Bridger-Teton National Forest map, Buffalo and Jackson Ranger Districts.

Finding the trailhead: From Moran Junction, travel 30 miles east on U.S. Highway 26/287 (toward Dubois) to Forest Service 515 on your left. A sign indicates it is the road to Brooks Lake. This point is 5.3 miles east of Togwotee Pass. Follow FS 515 for 5 miles to its end at the Yellowstone Trailhead, which is just beyond the campground.

Parking and trailhead facilities: Brooks Lake Campground (fee) has 14 sites, picnic tables, potable water, outhouses, and bear-proof refuse containers. There is room for several cars at the trailhead parking area.

Key points:

3.3   Meadows on Cub Creek.
13.0   South Buffalo Valley.
20.5   Pendergraft Meadows and ford of Lake Creek.
23.0   Lake Fork Falls.
25.0   Ferry Lake.
25.5   Soda Fork Trail junction.
26.0   Woodard Canyon Trail, Marston Creek Trail, and Soda Fork Trail junction. South Fork Loop and Yellowstone Meadows Loop hikers depart. South Fork Loop hikers return.
27.0   Unnamed pass. Yellowstone Meadows Loop hikers return.
28.0   Crater Lake.
31.0   Big Springs.
34.0   Nowlin Trail junction.
35.5   Upper Nowlin Meadow.
38.0   South Buffalo Trail junction.
41.7   Trail Creek.

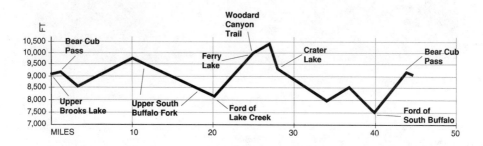

The hike: This popular and scenic loop traverses a number of habitats through dry lodgepole pine forests, deep river canyons, lakes, and alpine tundra. Begin by walking the 3 miles from the Yellowstone Trailhead to Upper Brooks Lake (Hike 8). From Upper Brooks Lake, the trail passes through mushy ground and climbs 0.3 mile to Bear Cub Pass, which is the Continental Divide and the Teton Wilderness boundary.

For 0.25 mile past the pass, you follow a narrow, gently downhill-sloping meadow enclosed by forest. A small creek starts in this meadow. Soon, however, the grade of the trail increases sharply. It drops 400 feet in an often muddy 0.5 mile that runs through deep forest. You emerge from the forest in a sloping meadow above Cub Creek. In a big mud hole at the start of the meadow, the trail forks. Take the right fork and head up Cub Creek on its south side. (It is surprising that the trail location on the Togwotee Pass and Dundee Meadows quad is completely wrong for the first 3 miles. The trail does not cross Cub Creek until the meadows before the word "Creek" on the Dundee Meadows quad.) The trail then crosses the top of the meadow and climbs steeply 0.25 mile into the forest. You emerge from the forest at 2.3 miles and pass the first of several small lakes.

At 3.3 miles, the trail comes to some meadows next to Cub Creek and shortly arrives at a lightly used outfitter camp. The trail finally crosses the creek just beyond the camp. Before long you drop down a bit and cross a mile-long meadow through which Cub Creek winds gracefully. Here you get some beautiful views of the plateau walls that rise nearly vertical on both sides of the canyon.

At 6 miles and 9,300 feet, the forest opens up and the climb gets noticeably steeper. Whitebark pine appears and so does grizzly sign. Elk and deer are seen here, too. The canyon gets narrower, and the nearly vertical canyon walls get lower. In season, the alpine wildflowers are astounding. At 8 miles, arrive at the 9,900-foot divide and enjoy the views down both Cub Creek and South Buffalo Canyons. The view of the Buffalo Plateau as you look back down the South Buffalo is reminiscent of the much-photographed Squaretop Mountain in the Wind River Range. The divide is broad, level, and grassy. From the divide, the trail bears faintly right and descends steeply, and after about half a mile, crosses the tiny South Buffalo in a large meadow. Continue south through the meadow and enter the tree line at 9.2 miles. The South Buffalo, much larger now, rages in a steep, narrow gorge, and the trail climbs quickly onto a ledge above it. Several small landslides have damaged the trail in this steep and narrow section.

At 10.5 miles, arrive at a large, flower-filled meadow at the bottom of the steep gorge. The dark walls of the Buffalo and Cub Creek Plateaus rise above you on three sides—a powerful view, especially in midsummer when the previous winter's snow cornices hang along the top of the plateaus, contrasting with the dark volcanic rocks. From here, the topography of the South Buffalo levels out. The trail climbs above the river for the next 2 miles, although your quad incorrectly shows it following rather close to the South Buffalo. It is steep, very wet, and has been highly eroded by horse traffic. Finally, you descend to a ford at 13 miles. Cross at a gravel bar 50 feet upstream. From here to Upper Pendergraft Meadows, you are enveloped by the wild and remote valley of the South Buffalo. Your Dundee Meadows quad also shows back-to-back fords in 0.5 mile. These do not exist. Your next ford is at Turner Fork, which is in another mile. Another gravel bar is 25 feet upstream from the trail. There are three channels of Turner Fork and three more fords of the South Buffalo within the next 2 miles. Look for the gravel bars! Half a mile beyond the third ford, you reach massive Upper Pendergraft Meadows, a popular site for outfitters. You will often encounter several parties and many horses here. There are also many offshoots of the trail here, so stay close to the river. At 18 miles, you arrive at a sign that says "trail," followed immediately by a ford. The gravel bar is 75 feet upriver.

Now you climb over a shoulder of Pendergraft Peak and drop into the Lake Creek canyon, which is almost as big as the South Buffalo. At 20.5 miles, arrive at the ford of Lake Creek at Pendergraft Meadows. This ford is the second most difficult ford of this loop. People have drowned at the trail crossing in high water. Instead, go upstream 0.25 mile to a gravel bar and cross, then pick your way through the deadfall back to the Lake Creek Trail and turn right. Lake Creek Trail heads northeast toward the wall of the Buffalo Plateau (about 1,400 feet overhead). Soon the trail enters the forest, crosses a number of small tributaries of Lake Creek, and then approaches its bank. After following Lake Creek for 0.25 mile, the trail makes a steep, 600-foot climb into Lake Creek Canyon. As you climb, it becomes more obvious that Pendergraft Peak (now to the south) is not a peak, but the side of a plateau. On the climb over, the lodgepole pine forest changes to dense fir and the small open places produce wildflowers, a lush growth of cow parsnip (favored by grizzly bears), and other large perennial forbs. A 400-foot-high vertical cliff hangs just over your head at the canyon's mouth.

If you walk down to Lake Creek, you are greeted with an awesome sight— the creek suddenly tumbles through a slot in the volcanic rock. The slot is only 3 feet wide, and the creek's waters plunge into a deep, green pool. From here the creek tumbles into another pool and then churns out of sight with a roar into a yawning chasm.

Back on the trail, you climb continuously, but at a moderate rate. The lower part of the canyon is narrow and filled with a dark forest. A number of tributaries cascade across the trail, providing ample drinking water. At 22.6 miles, the trail arrives at the ford of a major tributary of Lake Creek. At 23 miles, beautiful Lake Fork Falls tumbles about 40 feet into a pool and another ford. Past the falls, the trail switchbacks uphill 200 feet and comes to an unsigned fork in 0.5 mile. You bear left and climb a steep 700 feet to Ferry Lake in 1.5 miles. The outlet of Ferry Lake is spectacular, plunging immediately over a small waterfall, then another, and another—each bigger than the one before. The stream drops off the plateau to join Lake Creek at Lake Fork Falls 800 feet below.

The trail goes around the east side of Ferry Lake and reaches the signed Soda Fork Trail in another 0.5 mile. This is the return point for the South Fork Loop (Hike 11). Turn left and head east on the Soda Fork Trail. Within 0.5 mile, you arrive at the signed junction with the Woodard Canyon and Marston Pass Trails. This is the backcountry trailhead for both the Yellowstone Meadows (Hike 10) and South Fork (Hike 11) loops.

Now you climb steadily on the Soda Fork Trail to an unnamed pass at 10,150 feet and 27 miles. This is the return point for the Yellowstone Meadows Loop. The views of the Tetons and Soda Fork Valley are spectacular. Nestled in the ramparts of Soda Mountain is Crater Lake, 700 feet and only 0.5 mile below. Get ready for the knee-buckling, 1-mile descent to Crater Lake. There are unimpaired views of the Tetons, Crater Lake, Soda Mountain, and Smokehouse Mountain. It becomes obvious that the latter two are really not mountains at all. They are only arms of the Buffalo Plateau, extending at a 45-degree angle from each other with the canyon of the Soda Fork between them. Crater Lake is fairly large with an irregular shoreline. It sits at the very head of the canyon with its back to the steep slopes that plunge from the top of the Buffalo Plateau. The volcanic breccia near Crater Lake has been eroded into many odd and grotesque shapes. Don't be surprised if a moose darts out from behind one. Moose are common in the valley of the Soda Fork.

For the next 3 miles, you descend 800 feet to Big Springs (no reliable water on this segment). Big Springs is a spectacular place. Here the Soda

Ferry Lake on the Buffalo Plateau. LEE MERCER PHOTO

Fork runs full-blown out of the hillside amid meadows, patchy timber, and many wildflowers. You trek downstream through immense alpine beauty as the Soda Fork Trail takes you through several spectacular meadows. Across the meadows to the north, tower the cliffs, peaks, and battlements of massive Soda Mountain. The south side of the canyon presents a similar scene where Smokehouse Mountain thrusts skyward. Finally you leave the world of alpine meadows and Absaroka volcanics behind and enter thick forest.

At 34 miles, arrive at the signed junction with the Nowlin Trail. Turn left and follow a little stream downhill 0.25 mile to a ford of the Soda Fork. This is a tough ford and it's always high because of Big Springs. On the south side of the stream in a clearing is a Forest Service patrol cabin. Past the cabin you climb very steeply, 700 feet in 1 mile, before arriving at a broad, open summit with beautiful scenery. The damp meadow on the other side of the summit is Nowlin Meadow. You cross the top of the meadow on a slope and then climb briefly before arriving at giant Upper Nowlin Meadow. The trail keeps to the east side of Upper Nowlin Meadow, following a small stream briefly before climbing 50 feet to a small saddle between two hills. From here you drop 500 feet in 1 mile to the junction with the South Buffalo Trail, which you reach at 38 miles. Head downstream (west-southwest) on the South Buffalo Trail toward Cub Creek. Soon, you come to a fine view of Terrace Meadows and the sparkling, almost gentle, South Buffalo as it meanders through this mile-long expanse. Three quarters of a mile from Nowlin Trail, arrive at the signed junction with Cub Creek Trail. Turn sharply left onto Cub Creek Trail and reach a ford of the South Buffalo, the most difficult ford in this guide. If the water is high, it is dangerous and inadvisable. Worse yet, there is no gravel bar. Fording at the trail is the only option. After this ordeal, you start climbing steadily away from the South Buffalo. If you're cold from the ford, this will warm you up quickly. Within 0.5 mile, you get a good view of Terrace Meadows and the Tetons in the distance. Now climb very steeply, passing a small creek that goes dry by August. At 40.7 miles, you crest the timbered ridgetop and start a long, gentle descent towards Trail Creek and Holmes Cave Creek.

At 41.7 miles, cross Trail Creek near an outfitter camp and start a steep, but short, 400-foot climb. The trail heads southeast over rolling terrain. You hike through patches of spruce-fir forest with many openings that provide good views of the Simpson Peaks. Occasionally, you get glimpses of the volcanic walls of the Cub Creek Plateau rising overhead. The rock under-foot, however, is not volcanic. By its white, chalky texture you can see it's sedimentary.

Finally you start a long, 600-foot descent to the ford of Cub Creek, which you reach at 43.7 miles. From here climb 0.5 mile to the mud hole where the Yellowstone Trail heads south to Upper Brooks Lake. Retrace your steps to Brooks Lake.

Options: You can visit spectacular South Fork Falls by heading upstream (left) 0.5 mile from the Nowlin–South Buffalo junction to an unsigned trail on your right. Descend 0.3 mile to the falls. Water literally explodes through a series of narrow lava canyons.

Volcanic breccia in Cub Creek. RALPH MAUGHAN PHOTO

10 Yellowstone Meadows Loop

Highlights:	Beautiful and vast Yellowstone Meadows; Parting of the Waters Natural Landmark (Continental Divide); the spectacular and remote canyon of the Upper North Buffalo Fork; wildlife.
Type of hike:	Backpacking loop.
Total distance:	87 miles.
Difficulty:	Moderate.
Maps:	USGS Togwotee Pass, Dundee Meadows, Ferry Lake, Thorofare Plateau, Yellowstone Point, Two Ocean Pass, Joy Peak, and Crater Lake quads; Bridger-Teton National Forest map, Buffalo and Jackson Ranger Districts.

Finding the trailhead: The three-way junction of the Soda Fork, Marston Pass, and Woodard Canyon Trails is the backcountry trailhead for this loop. Refer to Hike 9, key point 26.0. This hike requires you do Hike 8 and Hike 9 as well.

Key points:

2.0	Descent down Woodard Canyon.
3.5	Ford of three unnamed streams.
4.5	Outfitter camp.
10.5	Castle Creek ford.
16.5	Hawks Rest Patrol Cabin and pack bridge over the Yellowstone.
18.0	Atlantic Creek ford.
21.5	Two Ocean Pass.
23.3	North Buffalo Fork Trail junction.
40.0	Soda Fork Trail.

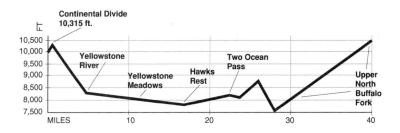

The hike: From the signed junction near Ferry Lake, the trail climbs steadily 1 mile to the Continental Divide and a sign that says, "Yellowstone Trail, Marston Fork." The view from the top is spectacular. As far as the eye can see are deeply incised volcanic plateaus. The spectacular ramparts of the mighty Thorofare Plateau (the largest, most remote, and most difficult-to-access plateau in the Teton Wilderness) dominate the scene beyond the Yellowstone River. Ferry Lake seems farther beneath you than it actually is. The Tetons are visible in the distance.

Yellowstone Meadows Loop
South Fork Loop

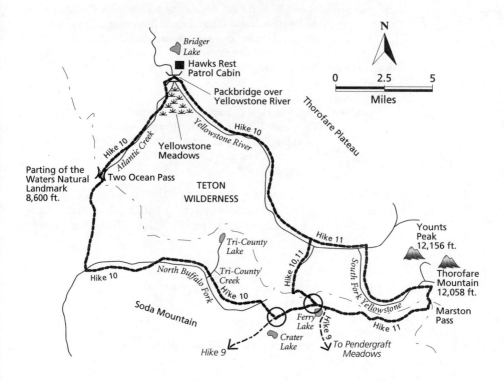

The trail begins its 4.5-mile, 2,000-foot descent to the Yellowstone River on new switchbacks down the east side of Woodard Canyon. At 2 miles, the descent steepens, and at 3.5 miles, you cross a series of three streams before getting a view of a magnificent waterfall tumbling over a set of convoluted breccia cliffs against a backdrop of snow cornices straddling the divide. From here, you continue to descend steeply to the Yellowstone River and a large and unsightly outfitter camp. You are now in a deep canyon with 800-foot walls towering above you. Ford the Yellowstone River—knee deep in late August—to reach the Yellowstone River Trail on the other side in a small meadow.

Head downstream and shortly enter the huge Mink Creek Fire Complex. This was one of the largest of the 1988 Yellowstone fires, but it received little or no publicity because it was deep in the wild heart of the Teton Wilderness, not threatening million-dollar condos or resort hotels. The trail starts climbing steeply around a spectacular lava gorge. At the top of the climb is a stunning view of this deep gorge. The torrent flows around a lava pinnacle in the middle of the river. The canyon is cloaked in forest, rich and lush, while a few scant feet away is an almost total burn. The contrast is startling. Descend steeply on the very narrow trail to a point where the canyon widens. At 6.5 miles, the trail arrives at a fine view of a large oxbow bend in the river. At 10.5 miles, arrive at the ford of Castle Creek and 0.5 mile later, pass a microburst-fallen forest to your right. At 12.5 miles, arrive at another oxbow bend in the Yellowstone that has a sandy beach next to a deep swimming hole.

From here, it is 4 more miles through the vast freshwater marshes of Yellowstone Meadows to the Hawks Rest Patrol Cabin and the pack bridge over the Yellowstone (one of the few bridges found in the Teton Wilderness). Stand here for a moment and survey the scene. You are enveloped by vast Yellowstone Meadows. It is a Pleistocene image that greets you here as birds such as sandhill cranes, bald eagles, hawks of all kinds, trumpeter swans, white pelicans, geese and innumerable species of ducks congregate in maritime numbers. This place conjures up images of the Yukon in the mind's eye. At dusk, moose wander out to feed. The specter of the grizzly looms large. After you cross the bridge, turn left and head for Two Ocean Pass on Atlantic Creek Trail, which heads across Yellowstone Meadows and begins its gradual climb to Two Ocean Pass in the burn.

At 18 miles, ford Atlantic Creek and enter its canyon. The creek meanders nearby, all the way to Two Ocean Pass, which you reach at 21.5 miles.

View eastward (down Atlantic Creek) from the nearly flat Two Ocean Pass, Teton Wilderness.
RALPH MAUGHAN PHOTO

Yellowstone River. LEE MERCER PHOTO

Two Ocean Pass is the Continental Divide, but it doesn't look at all like a pass. Instead it looks like a wet meadow with an almost imperceptible slope. It is unique because it drains toward both oceans. If you take the Two Ocean Trail, which leaves to the right on top of the pass, you'll soon come to Parting of the Waters Natural Landmark, where North Two Ocean Creek tumbles down from its source on the Two Ocean Plateau and splits into two streams at the base of a tree. One branch becomes Pacific Creek and one Atlantic Creek. A trout can actually swim over the Continental Divide here. A sign reads "Atlantic Ocean 3,488 miles, Pacific Ocean 1,353 miles."

From the Two Ocean Plateau Trail junction, follow Atlantic Creek Trail 0.5 mile to the signed junction with Pacific Creek Trail. Follow this to the North Buffalo Fork Trail junction, which you reach at 23.3 miles. Turn left. This trail is wide and heavily used by horses. From here you climb gently through meadows and burned forest as you follow tumbling Trail Creek. At 26.3 miles, reach Trail Creek Divide and enjoy the good views. From here you descend 800 feet in 3 miles, arriving at the faint unsigned trail up the North Buffalo Fork. It leaves to the left, at the bottom of the hill, at the site of a heavily used outfitter camp.

The heavy traffic on North Buffalo Fork Trail doesn't extend up the North Buffalo Fork. The upper reaches of the North Buffalo Fork are seldom used, and yet are very beautiful, especially above North Buffalo Fork Falls. The trail is in good condition to North Buffalo Fork Falls and in fair condition beyond. Fine wilderness campsites are almost unlimited to the end of the trail. The upper reaches of the North Buffalo Fork are notable for their many beautiful falls, cascades, and meadows set between towering plateau walls. Of the three forks of the Buffalo, we think the North Buffalo Fork has the best scenery. In short, this canyon is a backpacker's paradise.

The trail heads up the canyon and is an intimate footpath, a relief from the wide and horse-pounded North Buffalo Fork Trail you just left. Soon the forest openings cease, and you walk through riverside forest most of the way to North Fork Buffalo Falls at 33 miles. During the first 2 miles on the North Buffalo Fork Trail, side trails occasionally dart off to the right. Don't follow them; just keep heading up the canyon, which closes tighter around you as you go. North Fork Falls is a double falls, thundering down through a slot in the volcanic rock. A side trail leads to the falls, while the main trail climbs to a shelf above them. A large swimming hole at the base of the lower falls proved too cold to swim in when we were there. You don't see the falls from the main trail, but on the shelf you get a view back down the heavily forested canyon and your first unimpaired view of the rugged country in the upper canyon of the North Buffalo Fork.

Back on the main trail, a brief walk through the forest brings you to a large meadow (0.75 mile long) at 33.5 miles. This is the first of three such meadows between the falls and the top of the canyon. The trail crosses the North Buffalo Fork twice in the meadow, but these crossings are unnecessary. Use the game trails on the north side of the meadow to keep your feet dry. One and a half miles beyond the meadow's end, the canyon turns sharply south at the base of the walled mountain before you. This mountain is actually the Buffalo Plateau, as are the mountains to your right side. The bend southward comes at the crossing of a major tributary of the North Buffalo Fork–Tri-County Creek (unnamed on most maps). Tri-County Creek tumbles down a steep, rough canyon without a trail. Its origins are near the Continental Divide in a large and rarely visited lake that is unnamed on the Two Ocean Pass quad, but is called Tri-County Lake. It's located very near the point where Park, Teton, and Fremont Counties share a common boundary. The second of the upper North Buffalo Fork's meadows begins at the canyon's southward bend at the Tri-County ford. This meadow is long and sinuous. The trail follows the river closely. The walls of the Buffalo Plateau rise all about you in massive cliffs dotted with holes. At the end of the second meadow, at 36.5 miles, you are in for a steep climb of 450 feet, all of it through forest. At the top of the climb, you stride into the final of the three meadows, which is about a mile long. Here the North Buffalo Fork meanders through low willows, grass, and wildflowers. Look downstream from about the middle of the meadow to where a very impressive wall rises to the left. While you may not have noticed, the canyon has made another right-angle turn and is now heading eastward again. Past the meadow, the trail climbs steeply and continuously. The track begins to deteriorate, and the best scenery is yet to come. The trail finally peters out at timberline amid a beautiful, flowered slope at 38.5 miles. Cow parsnip, red and yellow monkeyflowers, Indian paintbrush, and many more blaze away in July and August, while the North Buffalo Fork's headwaters dash over black volcanic cliffs from their sources on the Continental Divide to form six beautiful waterfalls.

The route over to the Soda Fork Trail is simple. Almost due south is a break in the top of the cliff band. Head toward that break and gain the plateau. The wildflower display on top is simply incredible. Now look to your west and see a large cliff wall that is the head of a major tributary of the Soda Fork. A trail takes you around the base of that cliff wall and disappears on the other side in a large, grassy meadow. No matter, just head south about a third of a mile, and you will strike the Soda Fork Trail above Crater Lake at 40 miles.

11 South Fork Loop

See Map on Page 72

Highlights:	Some of the most spectacular scenery in the contiguous 48 states; isolation; wildlife.
Type of hike:	Backpacking loop.
Total distance:	70 miles.
Difficulty:	Moderate.
Maps:	USGS Ferry Lake and Younts Peak quads; Bridger-Teton National Forest map, Buffalo and Jackson Ranger Districts.

Finding the trailhead: The three-way junction of the Soda Fork, Marston Pass, and Woodard Canyon Trails is the backcountry trailhead for this loop. Refer to Hike 9, key point 26.0. This hike requires you do Hike 8 and Hike 9 as well.

Key points:
8.5	North and South Fork of the Yellowstone River.
8.9	North Fork ford.
12.0	South Fork ford.
16.0	Continental Divide.
17.0	Marston Pass.
17.3	Marston Fork Trail.
17.8	Buffalo Plateau.

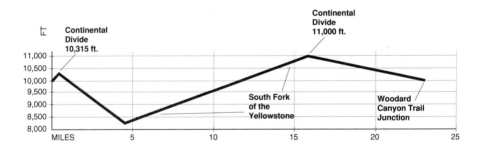

The hike: This hike is one of extraordinary beauty and scant use. Few people head up the South Fork of the Yellowstone toward the Continental Divide. If you like rugged mountain scenery, you should become one of those few. Continue up the Yellowstone River from the unsigned junction with Woodard Canyon Trail at 4.5 miles (See Hike 10). The trail passes mighty walls of convoluted volcanic rock and good views of Younts Peak before crossing over the Continental Divide and ending in the country immediately beneath Marston Pass.

From the junction, hike east along the Yellowstone River. The trail is vague and somewhat hard to follow in places. For the first 3 miles, the trail

77

Above the North Buffalo Fork on the way to the Soda Fork, Teton Wilderness. LEE MERCER PHOTO

closely follows the river, partly in forest and partly in meadows. At 8.5 miles, arrive at this majestic river's north and south forks. The Yellowstone River is the longest free-flowing (undammed) river in the contiguous 48 states. The North Fork of the Yellowstone is a deep and narrow-bottomed canyon with no trail. It originates at a small glacier on the north side of Younts Peak at 12,156 feet. The South Fork of the Yellowstone, by contrast, is a broad-bottomed canyon of lush meadows with steep side walls.

Ford the North Fork 0.4 mile above its mouth and climb steadily through forest into the canyon of the South Fork. Struggle along a narrow trail on the canyon's side slope, crossing many tributary streams. It is heavily eroded in some places and footing can be somewhat tricky. Follow this difficult side slope for 2 miles from the river's mouth before suddenly descending to a beautiful, broad, mile-long meadow, which you reach at 10.5 miles. The South Fork of the Yellowstone meanders lazily, while tremendous plateau walls rise on each side of the meadow as well as ahead (due to the canyon's bend). This is a spectacular location.

Gradually the canyon tightens and the meadow disappears. The trail follows the river closely for 1.5 miles before fording the South Fork at 12 miles. Now the trail climbs steeply, gaining 400 feet in less than 1 mile. At 13 miles, you emerge into the canyon's upper meadow, with a tremendous waterfall tumbling from it into the gorge. The upper meadow is at timberline and is quite marshy. Mosquitoes are horrendous, even in late August. We could only stand here a short time, as they bit us unmercifully. The wildflower display here is world-class. We also saw an entire herd of bighorn sheep come across this marshy meadow on their way to the country around Younts Peak. A sheep highway leads them there from the Continental Divide. The trail here becomes vague, and some care is required to follow it. The views of Younts Peak are tremendous. We came away with a special regard for this great peak. The walking is easy (except for the wetness) as you traverse the high country. The wildflowers continue to blaze and we saw several hummingbirds. At 13.5 miles, you leave the marshy meadow behind. The trail is very faint, and the key is to stay as close to the main fork of the river as possible for the next mile. Branches will break off as they pour down the face of Younts Peak, and the main drainage will get progressively smaller. At 14 miles, this upper canyon tightens. Stay on the right side of river and carefully pick your way upstream. We stopped and marveled that we had reached the remote headwaters of the great Yellowstone River, the Ganges of the American West. Gandhi would have been happy here amidst the flowers, cool high-mountain breezes, and spectacular scenery. At 14.5 miles, the trail starts to leave the canyon and climbs steeply toward the Continental Divide. Across the canyon, back-to-back cascades tumble off Younts Peak toward the tiny South Fork. You should be heading due east at this point. At 15 miles, you will see a low spot on the skyline with a mountain just to its right and a bigger mountain just to its left. The big mountain is 12,058-foot Thorofare Mountain—second highest in the Teton Wilderness. Although it is very tempting, don't go up there because you will cliff out at the impassable canyon walls of Younts Creek. Instead, climb steeply up the right side of the canyon wall and head for the

Near Marston Pass, Teton Washakie boundary. LEE MERCER PHOTO

lowest spot you can find, south-southeast. You come to a big, grassy divide with a good view at 16 miles. This is the Continental Divide and you are at 10,700 feet. Just past the divide, there is a glacial tarn. Climb to the right and above it and you will find a trail contouring along the steep headwaters of West Fork Creek. The views are incredible!

Circumnavigate the top of West Fork Creek and descend 400 feet to Marston Pass at 17 miles. This traverse requires an ice ax in some years, due to snow cornices that persist into August. The view eastward from Marston Pass is tremendous. In the Teton Wilderness, it is second only to Big Game Ridge. You have to walk just a short distance beyond the pass to get the full immensity of the scene. The vertical-walled sides of plateaus are visible in all directions. Eroded ridges support pinnacles, battlements, waterfalls, and permanent snowfields. Below, down in West Fork Creek and Marston Creek, the volcanic harshness is softened by green forest. The giant wall to the southeast is appropriately named Wall Mountain (elevation 11,498 feet). This escarpment, an edge of the Buffalo Plateau, drops almost 2,400 feet in a near-vertical sweep. In the distance, the mountain vastness of the Absaroka Range and the Washakie Wilderness goes on for as far as the eye can see. You are miles from any road and unlikely to meet a soul.

Now head west on the Marston Fork Trail. The Tetons come into view in the distance. To your south, Buffalo Plateau unfolds—a mighty geologic feature over 50 square miles in extent. The experienced backcountry adventurer can explore this land of small lakes, alpine tundra, stunted forests, and cliffs for days.

Three and a half miles west of Marston Pass, the trail finishes crossing the many headwaters of Lost Creek. The hill just to the north is the Continental Divide. A short climb from the trail will present you with a tremendous view of the canyon of the South Fork of the Yellowstone.

At 21.5 miles, pass the signed junction with the somewhat obscure trail to Lake Fork Trail. Just beyond, cross a large side stream and begin ascending the low saddle between the Lost Creek and Lake Creek drainages. Once on top, you pass through an area of krummholtz and descend to the Woodard Canyon Trail junction at 23 miles.

To return, follow Hike 9 from key point 26 back to the trailhead.

12 Jade Lakes

See Map on Page 64

Highlights: A short hike to two pretty, high-country lakes set beneath towering cliffs; good fishing.
Type of hike: Out-and-back day hike.
Total distance: 5 miles.
Difficulty: Easy.
Maps: USGS Togwotee Pass and Dundee Meadows quads; Shoshone National Forest map, North Half.

Finding the trailhead: About 27 miles west of Dubois on U.S. Highway 287/26 or 7.8 miles east of the Togwotee (toe-GUH-tee) Pass, Brooks Lake Road (FS 515) jogs north. This graveled main road is easy to follow for the 5.2 miles to the Brooks Lake Campground. Just before Brooks Lake Lodge, turn north at the campground sign, but don't enter the camping area. Stay west and drive the short distance to the signed trailhead near the south shore of Brooks Lake.

Parking and trailhead facilities: Brooks Lake Campground has 14 sites, picnic tables, potable water, outhouses, and bear-proof refuse containers. Room for several cars at trailhead parking area.

Key Points:
   2.0   Upper Jade Lake.
   2.5   Lower Jade Lake.

The hike: US 287 west of Dubois climbs into an absolutely enticing section of southern Absaroka high country. While driving, you notice that unusual, somewhat stratified layers of volcanic cliff keep bobbing into view. Upper and Lower Jade Lakes offer an easy 2.5-mile (one-way) hike that places you both directly under those naked cliffs and beside emerald lakes that reflect the majesty of the surrounding country. Jade, by the way, is Wyoming's official state stone.

The first 0.5 mile of trail follows the Yellowstone Trail, Trail 823 (Hike 8) to a sign pointing northwest to Jade Lakes. A new, relocated section of trail lets you avoid what used to be five or more eroded paths cutting up a steep hillside. Follow this uphill for a bit more than 0.5 mile. Then the walk mellows, and for the final 1.5 miles the path wanders through a gentle and more open forest.

The tiny, stagnant pond at 1.5 miles, although green in color, is not one of the Jade Lakes. Continue along the trail for another 0.5 mile and descend into a depression holding the beautiful, deep waters of Upper Jade Lake. Here, those layered Absaroka cliffs tower over and reflect off the lake's waters. Excellent camping is found near the lake's southwest shore and at its north shore by the creek outlet (100-feet-from-shore rule applies). Lower Jade Lake lies downhill 0.5 mile farther along the trail. It forms the big

Upper Brooks Lake Creek beneath the Breccia Cliffs and Jade Lake. RALPH MAUGHAN PHOTO

cousin of Upper Jade, but doesn't offer the cliff reflections or as many camping opportunities. Both lakes contain fish.

At the extreme northwest corner of the lower lake, a hunting trail cuts to the north. It appears to be an ancient Forest Service trail that they are trying to forget, and my advice is to help the Forest Service and don't follow it. I did walk the route, and it was a fun adventure until several miles later when I lost both the path and my sense of direction. I staggered back to Brooks Lake twelve hours later, having somehow traversed the untrailed Clear Creek drainage of the Teton Wilderness, an entire drainage away. This was a most humbling lesson on how even an experienced hiker can get confused and turn a simple hike into a lost-and-found situation.

13 Bonneville Pass

See Map on Page 64

Highlights: Outstanding views; lovely, flower-filled meadows.
Type of hike: Out-and-back day hike.
Total distance: 6 miles.
Difficulty: Moderate.
Maps: USGS Dundee Meadows quad; Bridger-Teton National Forest map, Buffalo and Jackson Ranger Districts.

Finding the trailhead: From Moran Junction, travel 30 miles east on U.S. Highway 26/287 (toward Dubois) to Forest Service 515 on your left. A sign indicates it is the road to Brooks Lake. This point is 5.3 miles east of Togwotee Pass. Follow FS 515 for 4 miles to the junction with FS 516. Bear right on FS 516 and follow it 1.5 miles to its end at Bonneville Creek. The trail begins at the crossing of Bonneville Creek.

Parking and trailhead facilities: There is primitive camping (no outhouses) and ample parking.

Key points:
- 1.5 Meadow, view of Jules Bowl.
- 2.5 Bonneville Creek.
- 3.0 Bonneville Pass.

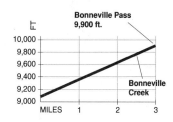

The hike: From the crossing, the trail heads upstream through a lovely, wet, spruce-fir forest. After 0.5 mile, it begins to climb noticeably. At 1.5 miles, you break out of the forest into a spectacular but steep meadow. Across the creek to the immediate south is awesome and forbidding Jules Bowl. A giant cliff wall that often contains a snow cornice until late summer towers above the basin of Jules Bowl. On either side are spectacular pinnacles and spires—the very landforms that give this area its name, the Pinnacle Buttes.

Now climb steeply, arriving at the open country just beneath Bonneville Pass, where you cross the now tiny Bonneville Creek at 2.5 miles. Cairns mark the trail the last 0.5 mile to Bonneville Pass. The pass is actually a grassy saddle, and makes an excellent lunch stop. The view is spectacular, encompassing all of the sublime country of the Pinnacle Buttes. The wall of the Continental Divide towers above the grassy openings of Dundee Meadows, 2,000 feet beneath you. Coffin Butte and the Ramshorn Peak are in the distance to the east.

Bonneville Pass. RALPH MAUGHAN PHOTO

14 Holmes Cave

See Map on Page 52

Highlights: Intimate and sublime views of the Breccia Cliffs. Holmes Cave is among the most interesting landforms (limestone-karst topography) in the Yellowstone ecosystem.
Type of hike: Out-and-back day hike or overnight backpack.
Total distance: 7 miles.
Difficulty: Moderate.
Maps: USGS Angle Mountain and Togwotee Pass quads; Bridger-Teton National Forest map, Buffalo and Jackson Ranger Districts.

Finding the trailhead: From Moran Junction, head east on U.S. Highway 26/287 (toward Dubois). After 19 miles, turn left onto a short dirt road that ends at a stock cabin (often occupied). Don't park right by the cabin. This is 5 miles east of Cowboy Village Resort (formerly Togwotee Lodge) and 4.5 miles west of Togwotee Pass.

Parking and trailhead facilities: Unimproved.

Key points:
1.5 Teton Wilderness boundary; top of Angle Mountain.

1.8   Unnamed creek crossing.
3.5   Unnamed stream; Holmes Cave.

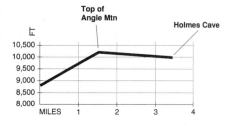

The hike: This hike begins at an elevation of 8,820 feet. The trail begins beside a fenced horse pasture and is often muddy, but it soon climbs up onto a bench. Moose are common. So are bears. The trail climbs generally to the north or northeast up the slopes of Angle Mountain, affording some good views of the Breccia Cliffs, the Tetons, and the gentle country to the south.

At 1.5 miles, you reach the Teton Wilderness boundary at a point on top of Angle Mountain (10,218 on your Togwotee Pass quad). The trail rounds this point and drops down into the big basin between Angle Mountain and the Breccia Cliffs.

At 1.8 miles, you cross an unnamed creek meandering through a beautiful meadow and climb 200 feet up to a pass between a hill to the north and the Breccia Cliffs. There are a lake and pond on this broad pass. The trail splits just 0.25 mile beyond the pass. You take the left fork, which leads to a stream flowing through another lovely basin. Soon after you reach the stream, at 3.5 miles, the water flows right into the hillside and down a steep, rubble-strewn hole—Holmes Cave. This dangerous, steep, and small opening leads into a major cave. Do not descend alone and then only with appropriate equipment.

View east along the southern boundary of the Teton Wilderness; Breccia Cliffs.
RALPH MAUGHAN PHOTO

Volcanic breccia beneath the north face of the Breccia Cliffs. RALPH MAUGHAN PHOTO.

Options: For an even more scenic approach to Holmes Cave that adds 2 miles to the total distance, continue 1.2 miles beyond the short dirt road turnoff on US 26/287 to FR 30020 and turn left. If you don't have a four-wheel-drive vehicle, park at Road Camp Draw. There is room for a few vehicles on the low hill just to the right of the creek and left of FR 30020. Hoof it up the often very muddy or dusty jeep road 1 mile to scenic Lost Lake, which has a brilliant blue color. Avoid following the jeep road that heads to the right (east) shortly after beginning your walk up to Lost Lake. At Lost Lake the unsigned, but obvious, foot trail leaves from the northwest side of the lake (near the end of the road). It crosses many upper tributaries of Road Camp Draw. This is abundant moose country with many low-growing willows. You hike uphill to emerge in a meadow with a short, breathtaking view of the Breccia Cliffs. Occasionally there are tantalizing views of the cliffs as you climb. Finally you break out into wildly scenic but weird meadow country strewn with huge chunks of breccia past which the trail winds. The breccia has fallen from Breccia Cliffs just above. The trail parallels the base of the cliffs leading northwest. The going is fairly level, then the trail drops a bit, and then climbs again. It becomes increasingly evident that the goal is a pass where the volcanic Breccia Cliffs meet the limestone of Angle Mountain. In about 2 miles from the Lost Lake Trailhead, you reach this pass at 10,200 feet elevation. There are fine views of the Breccia Cliffs, including both their dramatic south and west faces. You can see a long way to the north into the Teton Wilderness, especially toward Terrace and Smokehouse Mountains. To the west, the Tetons are plainly visible and to the south is the gentle Moccasin Basin country, which is great wildlife habitat when the cows are not too numerous. Whitebark pine graces the partially open ridgetop which seems like—and is—serious grizzly country. From the pass you drop steeply, but briefly, down into a lovely flower-filled basin with patches of timber. The downhill grade is gentle, and in the middle of the basin, just before crossing the perennial stream that flows through it, you meet with the main trail.

15 Buffalo Forks Loop

See Map on Page 52

Highlights:	Hike traces a fairly gentle and scenic route around the lower reaches of the Buffalo Fork country, including the intimate, scenic, and easy-to-follow 5.5-mile stretch of the old North Buffalo outfitter trail.
Type of hike:	Backpacking loop.
Total distance:	23.5 miles.
Difficulty:	Easy.
Maps:	USGS Angle Mountain, Togwotee Pass, Crater Lake, and Joy Peak quads; Bridger-Teton National Forest map, Buffalo and Jackson Ranger Districts.

Finding the trailhead: Drive east of Moran Junction on U.S. Highway 26/287 for 17 miles to Cowboy Village on the left. Go behind it and follow a good dirt road for 0.3 mile to Angles Trailhead. Keep right; don't follow the dirt road that continues down the hill. The trailhead is of moderate size and usually uncrowded.

Parking and trailhead facilities: Unimproved.

Key points:

2.0	Pack bridge over South Buffalo.
6.5	Terrace Meadows.
8.0	Nowlin Meadows–South Buffalo Trail junction.
10.0	Upper Nowlin Meadows.
12.0	Soda Fork Trail junction.
14.8	Soda Springs.
19.5	Meadow on outfitter trail.
20.0	South Buffalo Trail junction (unsigned).

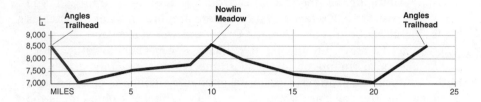

The hike: From the trailhead, follow the Angles Trail into the deep forest, and ignore a trail that you quickly reach to your left. The trail begins its descent slowly, but soon becomes steeper. After about 0.7 mile, you break out of the dense forest into steep side slope meadows with fine views of the west portion of the Teton Wilderness—Mount Randolph, Gravel Mountain, Gravel Ridge, and so on. At the edge of the meadows, the trail passes by big Douglas-fir and makes several steep, sweeping switchbacks to level out at a small meadow with a sign that marks a faint trail to your right, "Angles Cutoff Trail." This side trail is a shortcut up the South Buffalo Fork. It is useful to backpackers only late in the season in a normal water year because it leads to an otherwise difficult river ford. Past the cutoff trail, the main trail bumps up and down until it reaches the pack bridge across the South Buffalo Fork at 2 miles. Across the bridge is a sign at a T intersection trail junction that says "Turpin Meadows 4. South Fork Falls 9. Continental Divide 23." Turn right and head upstream on the South Buffalo Trail.

Now on this much busier trail, you quickly climb onto a heavily forested (lodgepole pine) bench above and away from the South Buffalo Fork. There are no views, but after 0.5 mile the forest begins to open a bit. The outfitter trail that is your return route exits faintly at an acute angle from the main trail. In another 0.5 mile, you cross a side stream. Just before you cross it, the trail splits. Both trails lead to the same place, but the lower trail goes out onto a gravelly flat along the river to avoid a steep side slope. Horse parties use the lower trail. The upper trail, which you take, climbs to avoid an oxbow of the river, of which you get a fine view. Both trails meet again where the canyon narrows, at 3.6 miles. The trail then closely follows the river. It is on your right and scenic cliffs rise to your left.

The constricted zone soon ends, and the trail crosses a small flat and then climbs 150 feet to a saddle at 4 miles, just to the northeast of point 7535 on your Angle Mountain quad. This climb is to avoid dropping into a river gorge (a very scenic gorge, however). Once beyond this pass, you begin to descend to the river again. As you approach the river, the Angles cutoff trail joins the main trail, and you come to a beautiful set of waterfalls, at which many parties stop. The falls are reminiscent of South Fork Falls far upstream.

Your stay at riverside is brief, for the trail climbs uphill again. It goes up a small defile, and is often muddy as you pass small cliffs amid dense thimbleberry ground cover. Then the trail levels out and goes through a deep forest of large conifers and dense thimbleberry understory—ripe in mid-August and sometimes full of bears. In this section you approach the South Buffalo

Fork several times. The river now flows placidly as you walk through the forest beneath the steep cliffs of Terrace Mountain to your left (north). Several times the river pushes the trail right to the edge of the cliffs and rock slides, and these points offer some fine views of the rugged limestone slopes of Angle Mountain on the south side of the South Buffalo Fork canyon. Finally, at 6.5 miles, you come to large, open Terrace Meadows with its fine views and great expanses. The trail heads directly across the meadows and into a conifer and willow forest. The trail is often muddy here. The unsigned Cub Creek Trail forks to the right at 7.5 miles. Just after this obvious junction, you steeply switchback up the side of a terrace. About halfway to the top you reach the signed Nowlin Meadows–South Buffalo Trail junction at 8 miles. Bear left and begin your climb to Nowlin Meadows. There is no water along the trail for some distance on this climb. Because Terrace Mountain consists of many limestone terraces and limestone is often as porous as a sponge, any surface water soon sinks.

At 9.2 miles, you reach a minor pass and drop down slightly to cross a tributary of County Line Creek. After this easy crossing, the trail follows the creek at a distance all the way to Upper Nowlin Meadows (10 miles), which is pretty, but not as scenic as Nowlin Meadows farther on. At Upper Nowlin you climb over some low ridges and then drop into beautiful Nowlin Meadows and a perfect view of Smokehouse Mountain.

After cutting across part of the meadow, the trail approaches timber as it climbs gradually to a nearly imperceptible pass. Over the pass, the trail begins its descent to the Soda Fork gradually. When it finally starts to de-

South Fork of the Buffalo. RALPH MAUGHAN PHOTO.

South Fork of the Buffalo River near its confluence with the North Fork. RALPH MAUGHAN PHOTO

scend in earnest, it does so steeply through a generally wet, north-facing forest. In places the trail is badly eroded. At the bottom you suddenly break out into a meadow with the Nowlin Meadow Patrol Cabin. At 12 miles, you reach the Soda Fork. The crossing here is very difficult in high water (3 to 4 feet deep and fast). Furthermore, the water level does not drop rapidly during the season because most of the Soda Fork's flow originates at a large, beautiful spring several miles upstream. The Soda Fork is a major stream. It usually has more volume than the North Buffalo Fork does at their confluence downstream in Soda Fork Meadows. Fortunately a large conifer fell across the Soda Fork in 1997. It provides a crossing, albeit a risky one in high water or if its surface is slick. Once across, the trail heads uphill and soon intersects the signed Soda Fork Trail. Turn left onto this trail and descend through lodgepole pine forest until you reach Soda Fork Meadows at 14.5 miles. It is another 0.3 mile to Soda Springs.

These springs are not great attractions like the thermal springs in Yellowstone. Nevertheless they gave the canyon its name. They are stagnant pools that slowly deposit travertine from solution. All the mountains nearby, including Soda Mountain, which rises immediately north of the springs, are made of limestone, the source of the calcium carbonate which is in solution. Carbon dioxide slowly bubbles out of the pools. If you look closely around the Soda Fork's riparian area, you will find other places where carbon dioxide is bubbling up from the ground.

Across the Soda Fork from the springs is a huge outfitter camp in a large set of meadows. Ford the Soda Fork and head west on an old outfitter trail.

This is the auspicious beginning of the North Buffalo outfitter trail. Following it is a little confusing here, as many trails develop. Follow the one that leads westward and gradually left past the wide mouth of the Soda Fork. At 16 miles, you pass a broken-down cabin on the left among large trees. The trail becomes fainter. Just stay on the east side of the North Buffalo Fork and you'll be fine. At 17.5 miles, the trail climbs gradually to a bench well above the North Buffalo. This is a fine stretch of trail to hike. There are usually lots of wildflowers, and little mud or trail erosion. The trail is well cleared, and you can make good time and enjoy a number of fairly good views. At 19.5 miles, you reach a meadow with a small spring. Within another 0.5 mile, you arrive at the unsigned junction with the South Buffalo Trail. Turn right and retrace your steps back to the Angles Trailhead.

Options: You can visit spectacular South Fork Falls by continuing upstream 0.5 mile from the Nowlin Meadows–South Buffalo junction to an unsigned trail on your right. Descend this trail 0.3 mile to the falls. Water literally explodes through a series of narrow lava canyons.

16 Bridger Lake

Highlights:	A pleasant journey to a lake that is the farthest linear distance from a road in the contiguous 48 states.
Type of hike:	Out-and-back backpack.
Total distance:	46 miles.
Difficulty:	Moderate.
Maps:	USGS Rosies Ridge, Angle Mountain, Joy Peak, Two Ocean Pass, and Yellowstone Point quads; Bridger-Teton National Forest map, Buffalo and Jackson Ranger Districts.

Finding the trailhead: From Moran Junction, head east 3 miles on U.S. Highway 26/287 to Buffalo Valley Road. Turn left and drive 10 miles to Turpin Meadows Campground on the left.

Parking and trailhead facilities: Turpin Meadows Campground (fee) has picnic tables, outhouses, bear boxes, and bear-resistant refuse containers. The trailhead is next to the campground. It is very large and has room for scores of vehicles, mostly horse trailers.

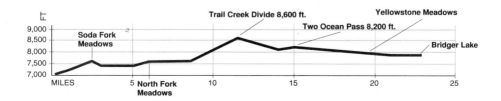

Bridger Lake

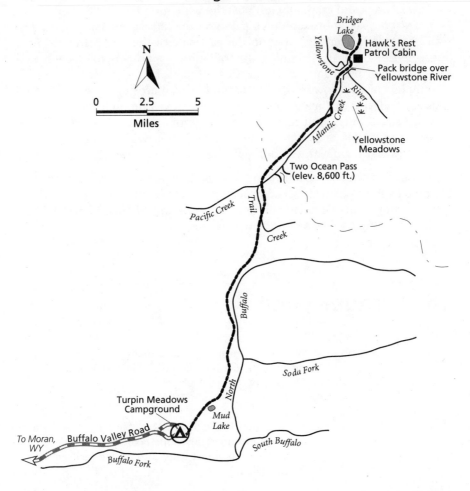

Key points:

3.0	Soda Fork Meadows.
4.0	Soda Fork Trail junction.
6.0	North Fork Meadows.
13.5	Pacific Creek Trail junction.
15.0	Two Ocean Pass.
18.7	Yellowstone Meadows.
21.0	Yellowstone River Trail junction.
23.0	Bridger Lake.

The hike: If you are seeking solitude, you should note that this is one of the busiest routes in the Teton Wilderness. In spite of this, it is a very pretty hike through lovely meadows on a well-maintained trail. The trail gets a lot of stock use, and it will turn soggy if there is extended rain. Elevation is gained and lost gradually throughout the trip.

From the trailhead, the North Buffalo Trail climbs gradually for 550 feet through aspen and lodgepole pine. At 2 miles, the climb ends at Mud Lake on the south side of the trail, and you begin a gradual descent to beautiful Soda Fork Meadows, which you reach at 3 miles. Throughout midsummer, wildflowers cover these meadows. The mountains you see to the east and northeast are the Absaroka Range. The North Buffalo Fork, which traces its way slowly through the meadow 0.5 mile to the east, forms the boundary between the Absaroka Range and the Pinyon Peak Highlands (burned in the Huck Fire) to the west. The Soda Fork Meadows are about 2 miles long and are broken up by patches of forest. The trail keeps to the meadows' west side. As you continue up the meadows, a large canyon comes into view toward the east. This is the Soda Fork Canyon. At 4 miles, you arrive at the junction with Soda Fork Trail. Do not take the Soda Fork Trail for this hike. Just past this point the meadows end and the canyon tightens. The trail avoids the canyon by climbing 400 feet to a saddle, then it drops into beautiful North Fork Meadows, which you reach at 6 miles. North Fork Meadows are wider and longer than Soda Fork Meadows. Sandhill cranes are commonly seen here. Their fantastic cries pierce the silence periodically. At North Fork Meadows, you enter the burn from 1988.

Bridger Lake with the Trident in the background. RALPH MAUGHAN PHOTO

At 9.5 miles, you arrive at an unsigned fork in the trail. The North Buf-falo–Two Ocean Trail is the left fork; the right fork is the North Buffalo Trail. You stay on the main trail (left) and continue on the North Buffalo–Two Ocean Trail. Climb steadily toward Trail Creek Divide, which you reach at 11.5 miles. You come to the headwaters of Trail Creek, then saunter gently downhill to reach Pacific Creek Trail at 13.5 miles. Turn right and walk this well-maintained trail to famous Two Ocean Pass at 15 miles. Turn right onto the signed Atlantic Creek Trail. The trail descends gently along meandering Atlantic Creek. At 18.7 miles, you ford Atlantic Creek (tough in high water) and enter massive Yellowstone Meadows. You are now engulfed by the massive Mink Creek Fire Complex.

At 21 miles, you arrive at the pack bridge over the Yellowstone near Hawks Rest Patrol Cabin and turn left on the Yellowstone River Trail. You arrive at a four-way junction at 22 miles. The two trails to the left lead to opposite ends of Bridger Lake. Both are 1 mile long. Both ends of Bridger Lake are extremely beautiful. It is not uncommon for many horse parties to be camped in the vicinity of the lake, so solitude is rare. But it is hard to call it overcrowded.

Absaroka Range

17 Five Pockets

Highlights:	A stunning mountain valley.
Type of hike:	Out-and-back day hike or backpack.
Total distance:	12 miles.
Difficulty:	Easy.
Maps:	USGS Five Pockets and Ramshorn Peak quads; Shoshone National Forest map, North Half.

Finding the trailhead: In the middle of Dubois, turn off Main Street at the bridge over Horse Creek onto the signed Horse Creek Road. The Horse Creek Road is paved until crossing the Little Horse Creek at 3.5 miles. Follow this road 5.5 more miles up Little Horse Creek to the Shoshone National Forest boundary. The road (now Forest Road 285) narrows at the forest boundary. In less than 1 mile, come to a junction with FR 511. Keep right on FR 285, and follow the road past ponds and down to a bridge over Horse Creek. You travel near Horse Creek around the boundary of a ranch. At 12 miles, reach FR 507 and turn left on this unimproved dirt road. Almost immediately you come to an optional trailhead, which is for use when conditions on the dirt road are bad (and they can be awful). If you think the weather will hold, drive down the dirt road about 2.5 miles to the second trailhead. Otherwise start hoofing it at the first trailhead. The trailhead is just a wide, grassy spot with no shade at the road's end.

Parking and trailhead facilities: Unimproved.

Key points:
- 2.5   Carson Lake.
- 3.5   Washakie Wilderness boundary; view of Cathedral Peak.
- 4.0   Horse Creek ford; view of Boedeker Butte.
- 4.4   Twilight Creek Trail junction.
- 5.5   Horse Creek ford.
- 8.0   Five Pockets.

The hike: The trail heads north as you leave the trailhead, passing a sign that reads, "Five Pockets." It winds gently downhill and meanders around for a while, but after about 0.7 mile, it begins to climb fairly steeply away from the stream valley, heading to the

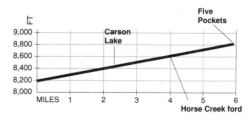

Five Pockets • Hidden Basin Loop • Emerald Lake
Frontier Creek • East Fork Loop

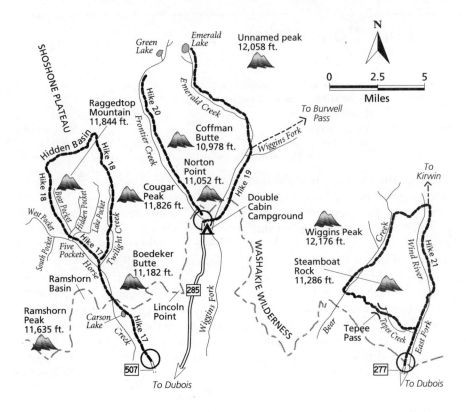

northeast. You might think this is the wrong trail because of the direction and the abundant unmarked trails that branch to your left (west). These are elk or angler trails. Avoidance of the gorge of Horse Creek is the reason for the climb. You gain about 500 feet in 0.5 mile. If you take the opportunity to scramble up the low limestone ledge to the left of the trail, the reward is a fine view of Horse Creek Canyon. Soon you level off and begin walking gently downhill. Small meadows appear, and at 2.5 miles, you come to Carson Lake—a shallow, scenic lake where moose like to hang out. You cross a nice spring that bubbles across the trail as you swing around the right side of the lake. Past the lake, you continue downhill briefly and then uphill for a combined distance of 0.5 mile. For another mile you ramble though forest and small meadows (there is one fair overlook of Horse Creek) and then reach the Washakie Wilderness boundary (signed) at 3.5 miles. Right at this point you get your first good view of a cathedral-like peak named (oddly enough)

"Cathedral Peak." So impressive from here, in reality it is just the eroded snout of a vast plateau. About 0.5 mile past the wilderness sign, you must ford Horse Creek. The ford is a bit swift, a bit deep, and it can be slippery—tough until midsummer. At the ford you get your first good view of big-cliffed Boedeker Butte to the east. This is a local landmark, especially visible to travelers on the forest roads below the Washakie Wilderness. Now safely across Horse Creek, tramp out into a small linear meadow. Head uphill through the meadow and enter a deep forest. At 4.4 miles, you reach the junction with the signed Twilight Creek Trail. Stay to the left for Five Pockets. After a brief climb followed by a short descent, there is a big change in scenery as you enter the beautiful, open, meadow country beneath Cathedral Peak. From here on, spectacular scenery is continuous. Just after entering this open country, you ford Horse Creek again. This time the creek is slow moving—a fairly easy ford although the water is moderately deep. The ford completed, saunter up the trail to arrive at the lower end of Five Pockets in just 0.5 mile.

Five Pockets is a beautiful, roughly oval valley enclosed for about 270 degrees by the huge volcanic ramparts of the Absaroka Mountains. The name comes from the five box canyons, or "pockets," that form the semicircle around the valley. Actually there are six pockets if you count a minor one between South and West Pockets. Your initial view is of just two of the pockets—Lake Pocket to your right and Bear Pocket ahead. The others become visible as you advance upstream. In addition to Horse Creek, numerous spring-fed brooks and their small tributaries meander across Five Pockets'

August snow flurry over Cathedral Peak from Horse Creek. RALPH MAUGHAN PHOTO

Five Pockets. Washakie Wilderness. RALPH MAUGHAN PHOTO

grassy and flower-filled meadows. Opportunities for photography are abundant, ranging from the different hues of meadow grass and flowers to the surrounding huge mountains. Good places to camp are plentiful, although some of the best are usually taken by outfitters. You should think about insects—biting flies and mosquitoes—when choosing your location. The wet parts of the meadow can generate clouds of flying, biting critters.

At 6 miles, reach the end of the trail near the entrance to Bear Pocket.

Options: There is quite a bit to do in Five Pockets. All of the pockets have at least game trails leading up them. These are not easy routes to follow, but persistence will yield rich rewards of scenery. Lake Pocket, the longest box canyon, has a partially maintained, unofficial trail that is quite easy. The terminus is at Lake Pocket Lake, situated in the tundra beneath unclimbable cliffs

18 Hidden Basin Loop

See Map on Page 96

Highlights:	The veteran wilderness enthusiast can use Bear Pocket to continue the Five Pockets hike (Hike 17) and make it into a bold, scenic loop.
Type of hike:	Backpacking loop.
Total distance:	26.4 miles.
Difficulty:	Difficult.
Maps:	USGS Five Pockets quad; Shoshone National Forest map, North Half.

Finding the trailhead: Begin at the end of the Five Pockets hike (Hike 17). Enter Bear Pocket.

Parking and trailhead facilities: Unimproved.

Key points:

5.0   Hidden Basin.
9.0   Junction with Twilight Creek Trail.

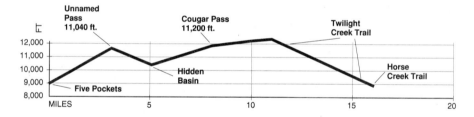

The hike: Once you've entered Bear Pocket, keep to the left of the stream and follow game trails through rough, but not impassable, country. The canyon broadens and the view opens up as you gain altitude. Bear Pocket has a very impressive wall at its head, but you can get around it by taking the right fork as you approach the wall. Then pick your way upward more than 1,000 feet to the pass at just over 11,000 feet and 3 miles. From the pass, the view of the Shoshone Plateau to the north is glorious. You can easily climb the mountain to your left (west), but the only route down is directly on the other side of the pass. A prudent person would bring an ice ax and crampons because a steep snow patch lingers late (pretty much all year). The main route drops into a cold-looking tarn 300 feet below. Once down, hike over near timberline and past a small lake until you reach Hidden Basin and the Cougar Pass Trail at 5 miles. Fill your water container at the springs here, because once you leave Hidden Basin it is many waterless miles to Twilight Creek.

Follow the Cougar Pass Trail to the right and begin your 1,300-foot ascent to the big, nameless plateau to the east. The trail switchbacks up the plateau

The Shoshone Plateau from near Cougar Pass. RALPH MAUGHAN PHOTO

side and reaches timberline at 10,400 feet. The views are good all the way, and those of Hidden Basin, the peaks near Raggedtop Mountain to the southwest, and gigantic Shoshone Plateau on the other side of East Fork Creek to the west just keep getting better. You suddenly reach the top of the plateau's north end at a snowfield that tumbles off into an abyss. Here the trail soon fades out in the tundra. Look for poles and cairns, which will lead to the signed junction with the Twilight Creek Trail at 9 miles. Head south, climbing gradually and following cairns and poles that have been placed sporadically.

As you approach Twilight Creek and the 11,642-foot-high point of the plateau, avoid the temptation to go right. Right leads to a view over huge, rotten cliffs down into Lake Pocket. Keep left and descend the now visible trail into Twilight Creek. Here you are so far above timberline that you can hardly see the trees (timberline is 3 miles farther down Twilight Creek). The roar of the wind is intense here; it sounds like a jet engine only yards away or perhaps a roaring beast. You probably won't reach water until you are 1 mile down Twilight Creek.

As you continue, the descent steepens, but the trail is good. There are no trailside views of Twilight Falls, which is a feature difficult to get a good look at. After a short, steep descent and a few short climbs, you finally reach Horse Creek at a fairly easy ford. Shortly after crossing the creek and climbing up into the forest on the other side, you reach the Horse Creek Trail at 16 miles. Turn left and retrace your steps 4.4 miles back to your rig.

Options: From Hidden Basin, you can climb Shoshone Plateau. It is a fine day hike with spectacular scenery and wildlife viewing opportunities. You could spend an entire day wandering this vast escarpment. The rock formations and the lichen clinging to them are sublime, and the late afternoon light is not to be missed.

You can also reach Hidden Basin from Hidden Pocket. For the Hidden Pocket route, enter Bear Pocket on its far right flank. Hidden Pocket is indeed hidden from most viewpoints in Five Pockets. It joins Bear Pocket at an acute angle near Bear Pocket's mouth. Keep to the right and above Bear Pocket Creek. Follow the numerous game trails through the forest. By doing so you automatically enter Hidden Pocket, rather than Bear Pocket. Be sure to keep out of the drainage bottom even if an elk trail leads to the creek, as it is really tough going down there.

Hidden Pocket's wall is not at its head, but on its left (west) side. At about 10,000 feet, glorious, flowery meadows appear amidst the whitebark pine and subalpine fir. Small tributaries enter, often with waterfalls. At timberline (elevation 10,200 feet) you get a good view down canyon and to the Wind River Mountains beyond to the south. As you near the top of Hidden Pocket, notice the more definite fork in this canyon than in Bear Pocket. You may be tempted to take the right fork because it looks gentler. It is not. The right fork is walled in at its top. Walk up the left fork, to a low, sloping wall with water trickling down its sides. The way to get past the wall is not to climb the rotten volcanic rock, but to move to the boulder field just to its left. Keep just left of the small stream there. You are directly beneath 11,800-

View north from the high pass between Hidden Pocket and Hidden Basin. RALPH MAUGHAN PHOTO

foot Raggedtop Mountain. Carefully climb through the boulders until you reach the bench above the wall. From here it's an easy walk to the pass. I noticed that a large number of flat rocks had been overturned and moved— bears, I figured. There was no recent bear scat, however. The pass is at 11,250 feet, and like the pass at Bear Pocket, there is a sublime view of the Shoshone Plateau and Hidden Basin below.

Now for the descent. In July it will be a snowfield. In August, I descended a steep slope covered with small, irregular rocks. You can't slide safely, but must pick your way down carefully. Then I came to a snowfield. In August, it was steep for a brief distance and then leveled a bit. Next came a pool of water and a small stream, then another, easier snowfield. I could then walk out into an untrammeled, untraveled meadow and sparsely timbered area. I stood beneath huge nameless peaks (except for the biggest one—Raggedtop).

Continue to walk downhill, to find the trail in Hidden Basin.

19 Emerald Lake

See Map on Page 96

Highlights:	Isolation; wildlife; spectacularly sculpted buttes, pinnacles, and battlements that are excellent examples of Absaroka volcanics. Emerald Lake is one of the few lakes in the Absaroka Range.
Type of hike:	Out-and-back backpack.
Total distance:	24 miles.
Difficulty:	Moderate.
Maps:	USGS Snow Lake and Emerald Lake quads; Shoshone National Forest map, North Half.

Finding the trailhead: In the middle of the town of Dubois, turn off Main Street at the bridge over Horse Creek onto the signed Horse Creek Road. Horse Creek Road is paved until you reach the crossing of Little Horse Creek at 3.5 miles. Follow the main road, which is now a good gravel road. It is 5.5 more miles up Little Horse Creek to the boundary of the Shoshone National Forest. The road (now Forest Road 285) narrows at the forest boundary. In less than 1 mile, you come to a junction with FR 511. Keep right on FR 285 and follow the road past ponds and down to a bridge over Horse Creek. You travel near Horse Creek around the boundary of a ranch. At 12 miles, reach FR 507, bear right, and continue on FR 285. At 14 miles, the road forks. Bear right again. Finally, at 27 miles, the road ends at Double Cabin Campground. The trailhead is down the hill on the left, near Frontier Creek at the trailhead signboard and register.

Parking and trailhead facilities: Double Cabin Campground (fee) has 15 sites, outhouses, potable water, and bear-proof refuse containers. To the left, in the giant meadow next to the trailhead, is unlimited primitive camping.

Key points:

0.1   Frontier Creek ford.
0.5   Wiggins Fork ford.
2.3   Washakie Wilderness boundary.
3.2   Fire Creek ford.
4.4   First Wiggins Fork ford.
5.0   Emerald Lake Trail junction.
7.7   Sheep Creek Canyon.
9.2   Emerald Creek ford.
12.0 Emerald Lake.

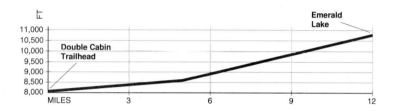

The hike: The trail up Wiggins Fork leaves the machine culture behind rapidly as it ascends an extraordinarily wild and unique valley that affords you an unprecedented look at Absaroka volcanics. Between the trailhead and Emerald Lake are nine fords, none of which are particularly easy. Sandals and a walking stick are a must. This hike is not a good choice during wet periods. The trail becomes gumbo and is very slippery. After a few falls, you're covered with mud and the smile has disappeared from your face.

The signed trail up Wiggins Fork fords Frontier Creek immediately, passes a small Forest Service guard station, and arrives at the wide, cold, swift ford of Wiggins Fork at 0.5 mile. Walk due east across the floodplain and Wiggins Fork Trail will reappear. Head upstream. The trail climbs gradually through lodgepole pine forest. Every so often the intricate columnar joints of Crescent Top appear to the west. At 1.5 miles, walk through an old burn from the 1952 fire. You reach the Washakie Wilderness boundary at 2.3 miles. At 3.2 miles, you cross Fire Creek on slippery rocks and at 4.4 miles, you arrive at a ford of Wiggins Fork. Keep those sandals on, because you ford back across at 4.6 miles. At 5 miles, you ford Wiggins Fork again and reach the signed junction with the Emerald Lake Trail. Go straight and begin the ascent to Emerald Lake along the Emerald Creek drainage.

Emerald Creek is a spectacular, wild, and remote drainage. The scenery gets bigger with every step. You have four fords in the next 2.5 miles. At 7.7 miles, incredibly vast, Alaskan-scale Sheep Creek Canyon opens up across Emerald Creek. Now enter a unique limber pine forest as you continue to ascend, ever more steeply, over an increasingly rugged footway. At 9.2 miles, reach the final ford of Emerald Creek.

You arrive at timberline at 11 miles. The trail disappears. No matter, the obvious route is a steep climb up to the cirque that contains Emerald Lake at 12 miles. Emerald Lake is an incredible place. In late July, all varieties of

View up the Wiggins Fork. RALPH MAUGHAN PHOTO

alpine wildflowers carpet the vast meadows that surround this shallow gem. The Absaroka Mountains tower above you in sheer walls of more than 1,000 feet. Sometimes, large herds of elk browse these meadows and their bugling pierces the air. Bighorn sheep are seen here as well as grizzly bears. I saw a large boar here in the summer of 1995.

Options: To combine the Emerald Lake and Frontier Creek hikes into a challenging, 25-mile loop, pick your way up the steep slope to the west of Emerald Lake. That little saddle between peaks 11656 and 12025 on your Emerald Lake quad is where you're headed. Crampons and an ice ax are helpful when the slope is snowy. It's a tough 1,700-foot climb in less than 1 mile and takes almost two hours with a full pack. Switchback up the hill to reduce exposure and fatigue. Once on top (the view is incredible), an old outfitter trail appears and takes you down to the headwaters of Frontier Creek, 11.5 miles upstream from the Double Cabin Trailhead.

20 Frontier Creek

See Map on Page 96

Highlights: An easy hike up a lovely canyon.
Type of hike: Out-and-back day hike or backpack.
Total distance: 18 miles.
Difficulty: Easy.
Maps: USGS Snow Lake and Emerald Lake quads; Shoshone National Forest map, North Half.

Finding the trailhead: See the Emerald Lake hike (Hike 19) for directions.

Parking and trailhead facilities: Double Cabin Campground (fee) has 15 sites, outhouses, potable water, and bear-proof refuse containers. It is at the end of FR 285 on the right. To the left, in the giant meadow next to the trailhead, is unlimited primitive camping.

Key points:
    0.5 Frontier Creek ford.
    7.0 Cougar Pass Trail junction.
    9.0 Frontier Creek ford.

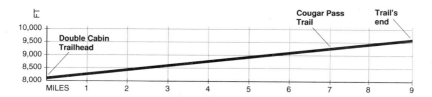

The hike: Day hikers can follow this route as far as they like. Backpackers have a host of options. This is a good trip for beginners.

From the sign at the trailhead, the Frontier Creek Trail heads north across the meadow. Within 0.5 mile, it crosses Frontier Creek and enters lodgepole pine forest, where it begins a long, almost unnoticeable ascent. The lodgepole pine gives way to Douglas-fir and Engelmann spruce after about 5 miles. You reach the signed junction with Cougar Pass Trail at 7 miles, 0.5 mile beyond a small meadow. From here, the trail continues upstream, with occasional good views of the narrowing and increasingly dramatic canyon of Frontier Creek. The trail ends at 9 miles at a ford where the canyon turns sharply east.

Options: You could establish a base camp near the junction with Cougar Pass Trail and do two spectacular day hikes. Add two days out and back from the trailhead and you have a relatively easy (by Absaroka Range standards) and rewarding four-day trip.

The first day hike is to Cougar Pass—3 miles and almost 3,000 feet on the Cougar Pass Trail. After 2 miles of stiff climbing, the trail reaches the tree

Norton Point near Double Cabin at the south boundary of the Washaskie Wilderness.
RALPH MAUGHAN PHOTO

line in a large and sublime basin with good views of the intricately sculpted volcanics of Crescent Top. From here, the trail bears left and ascends on highly eroded switchbacks to the top of Cougar Pass, actually an expansive plateau. Often, a snow cornice persists here until late in the year. You can usually pick your way around it. The area around Cougar Pass is expansive and you could spend an entire day exploring it. Bighorn sheep frequent this area. Maybe you'll see some. Return to your camp the way you came.

For the second day hike, follow Frontier Creek Trail to where the "official" trail ends, at the ford described above. From here, a much less used outfitter trail will take you 2 more miles to the basin that contains Green Lake, as well as another, unnamed lake. This is a spectacular location and not typical of most of the Absaroka Range. The hike is a stiff, 1,400-foot climb on a poor trail, but at least it's accompanied by diverting scenery. Return to your camp the way you came.

21 East Fork Loop

See Map on Page 96

Highlights: A challenging and adventurous loop into some of the most spectacular country in the Absaroka Range.
Type of hike: Backpacking loop.
Total distance: 27 miles.
Difficulty: Moderate.
Maps: USGS East Fork Basin, Dunrud Peak, Wiggins Peak, and Castle Rock quads; Shoshone National Forest map, North Half.

Finding the trailhead: From Dubois drive east on U.S. Highway 26/287 for 10 miles to the signed East Fork Road and turn left (north). This country recalls southern Utah with its fins, needles, and hoodoos. This is actually Chugwater formation, the calling card of Lake Bonneville. The gravel road you're on is a good one, and it bypasses many ranches en route to the East Fork Trailhead. After 10 miles, arrive at a fork. Turn right at the sign that says "Shoshone National Forest." After 15 miles, the road descends into a rather large valley where the Bitterroot Ranch is located. At 16.3 miles, pass under the Bitterroot Ranch sign, turn left at another sign that says "Shoshone National Forest," and ascend a steep hill on a rough road that can turn to impassable gumbo in wet weather. Follow this road 3 miles to the top of a pass and come to a fork that is signed "Bear Creek, East Fork." Go straight 2.7 miles to the East Fork Trailhead.

Parking and trailhead facilities: Primitive camping and ample parking for several cars.

Key points:
- 2.0   Junction with Tepee Creek Trail.
- 5.3   East Fork of East Fork.
- 9.7   Junction with Coal Chute Pass Trail.
- 12.0   Saddle between East Fork and Bear Creek drainages.
- 13.5   Junction with Bear Creek Trail.
- 20.0   Junction with Tepee Creek Trail.
- 22.0   Tepee Pass.
- 22.7   Tepee Creek.
- 25.0   Junction with East Fork Trail.

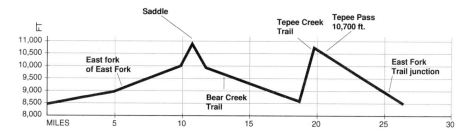

The hike: From the parking area at the East Fork Trailhead, the trail ascends a short lodgepole-pine bench to circumnavigate a short, tight section of the canyon of the East Fork of the Wind River. Within 200 yards it descends to a large meadow full of willows, where moose are a common sight. Look straight ahead to the north. The high mountains you see are where you're headed. Luckily, the East Fork Trail takes you there gently. It's well graded and well maintained.

At 2 miles, arrive at the junction with the Tepee Creek Trail, which is also your return route. In mid-July the forest floor is a sea of wildflowers—Indian paintbrush, lupine, columbine, phlox, fleabane, bluebell, arrowleaf balsamroot, and arnica, just to name a few. At 3.7 miles, you come to a meadow where the trail forks. Take the left fork, as the right one is very wet and leads to an outfitter's camp. In about another seven-tenths of a mile the the trail forks again. Bear left onto the fork that ascends the side hill. At 5 miles, you reach the ford of the East Fork. A sign at the ford says "East Fork Guard Station 6, East Fork Pass 7." If the river is high, go downstream 50 feet and cross in a shallow channel. Three-tenths of a mile beyond the ford, come to the East Fork of East Fork, denoted by a sign in a grassy meadow. At 6.3 miles, you come to a meadow with an outstanding view of East Fork Pass. The trail is cairned now and follows the valley upstream. Here you get your first taste of what is to come—the alpine universe of the high Absaroka. At the end of this meadow, cross a rather large stream. On the Dunrud Peak quad this is the one with the large drainage basin that is east of the "d" in "Wind."

During the next 3 miles you enter a world of perpetual alpine meadows only occasionally broken by stands of whitebark pine and subalpine fir. Sagebrush and, in July, wildflowers carpet the grasslands all around you. The magnificent East Fork Trail takes you to the high country as gently as possible. Other than the effects of altitude, you hardly know you're climbing. Every twist and turn of this trail contains hidden treasures in scenery and no amount of film for your camera is enough. We were overwhelmed by the color that extended like massive fingers as far as the eye could see wherever there was grass.

At 9.3 miles, cross a small side canyon, turn sharply right (east-northeast), and ascend beyond a small stand of whitebark pine. The trail then turns sharply left, levels out, and arrives at the signed Coal Chute Pass Trail junction at 9.7 miles. The East Fork is a classic alpine drainage now—at or above timberline. Magnificent, loud waterfalls tumble off Nine-Mile Mountain to the west, and towering peaks surround you in this spectacular place.

One hundred yards past the Coal Chute Trail is the signed junction with the Nine-Mile Trail. Turn left (west) and descend on switchbacks to the East Fork, which you reach at 10 miles. You can rock hop across, even in fairly high water. The Nine-Mile Trail looks like an erosion ditch coming through the whitebark pine on the west shore. It follows a drainage to the west, climbing steadily, and in 150 yards switches back to the right and then climbs 210 degrees southwest. It is marked by infrequent cairns and can be vague at times. At 10.3 miles, at a small meadow, it disappears. Look 210 degrees southwest through the whitebark pines uphill from a big clump of subalpine fir and you'll see it. At 10.8 miles, reach a side trail to a high viewpoint of East Fork, the Wind River Range, and the Continental Divide. This trail is not shown on your Dunrud Peak quad, but is the "peninsula" that has 10,776 at its southernmost point.

At 11 miles, you reach the top of little-traveled Nine-Mile Mountain with its crystal intrusions, spectacular Absaroka volcanics, glacial tarns, permanent snowfields, and giant elk herds. Cross a small stream at 11.5 miles. After this the trail disappears entirely. Get out your binoculars and glass 200 degrees south-southwest. You'll see a cairn between two subalpine firs about half a mile away and just beyond the cairn, a signpost. Head to that signpost, where you'll want to take the Nine-Mile Spur Trail to Bear Creek, which goes off 330 degrees northwest—an extremely sharp right, to say the least. The spur trail climbs to 10,739 on your quad, which is the divide between East Fork and Bear Creek. Often there is a snow cornice until late in the year that blocks the trail. You can go around it to the left. You reach the divide at 12 miles. A sign points to Bear Creek, a massive drainage whose upper reaches are visible 2,000 feet beneath you. The view on top of this divide is superlative, with much of the high Absaroka Range visible all around you. Mount Burwell, Dunrud Peak, Dollar Mountain, and Francs Peak are all visible to the northwest. The stunning flanks below Coal Chute Pass are visible to the east and are very impressive when being struck by lightning. Steamboat Rock is so close it looks as if you can almost touch it. An impressive high plateau beneath Wiggins Peak towers to the west.

Wiggins Peak above Bear Creek. LEE MERCER PHOTO

Now keep your eyes peeled for the cairns that mark the descent to Bear Creek. After 0.5 mile, you cross a stream and pass a small outfitter camp in a clump of subalpine fir. Below the outfitter camp, the trail is clearly defined as it enters whitebark pine and continues its steep descent. Finally, at 13.5 miles, reach the Bear Creek Trail, turn left (south), and head downstream. The views up and down the canyon are extraordinary. The wildflower display in July and August is fantastic with white and red Indian paintbrush, lupine, fleabane, spring beauty, gentian, phlox, and many more to delight the eye. The canyon tightens considerably after 0.2 mile. Huge breccia cliffs create a spectacular scene on the west side of Bear Creek. Waterfalls tumble down through the spires, creating a truly dramatic effect. The small meadows the trail passes through on the east side are a continual sea of wildflowers. Beargrass and elephant head appear below tree line.

The trail now climbs high above Bear Creek and at 14 miles, you pass a lovely side canyon with a misty waterfall, which provides a fine microhabitat for a multitude of wildflowers, including elephant head, pink gentian, red Indian paintbrush, and bluebell.

The trail continues to ascend, with increasingly dramatic effect. At 14.8 miles, come to a T intersection. Bear left and continue downstream. Half a mile later you come to another side stream in a small canyon. Notice the layer of lava in between the two layers of conglomerate in the canyon wall.

Finally, at 16 miles, the canyon opens up. The trail is now running on a contour several hundred feet above Bear Creek. At 16.3 miles, come to a beautiful side canyon with lovely waterfalls. A walk upstream here reveals a narrows and a box canyon with a giant waterfall. A quarter of a mile farther you'll come to a giant conglomerate outcrop on your right. At the foot of it is a faint side trail. Follow it 150 yards to a spectacular view of Bear Creek Canyon, as well as a large side canyon draining the country around Wiggins Peak. At 17.5 miles, you reach the ford of Bear Creek. The trail on the other side is cairned. You ascend away from Bear Creek and enter a large, sage-filled meadow. The trail goes up and down along Bear Creek for the next 2 miles. At 19.5 miles, reach a meadow on a high bench with fine views. Look downstream and see a giant conglomerate boulder that fell off the plateau above and landed in the icy waters of Bear Creek thousands of years ago. It is also a landmark that indicates you are near Tepee Creek Trail. You descend through lodgepole pine and aspen and arrive at the trail junction at 20 miles. The climb up this unnamed mountain via Tepee Creek Trail is arduous, to say the least. It gains 1,900 back-breaking feet in 2 miles. To make matters worse, you do not see water again for 2.7 miles. "Camel up" and carry extra water.

The trail ascends immediately as it leaves Bear Creek, climbing for 0.5 mile far above a small side canyon with a tumbling stream. The trail switch backs left and leaves the little canyon, continuing its relentless climb through lodgepole pine, Douglas-fir, and Engelmann spruce. At about six-tenths of a mile, a bench is reached with a good view of Bear Creek. Note how far you've climbed already. Continue to ascend now via steep switchbacks. At 21 miles, you reach what is functionally the tree line and at 22 miles, you arrive at the top. The spires of Castle Rock tower above you to the south. Steamboat rises just as dramatically to the north. Wiggins Peak scrapes the sky at more than 12,000 feet to the west. Crescent Top near Wiggins Fork is in view, as is Younts Peak and much of the Absaroka Range, as well as Gannett Peak, Fremont Peak, and Titcomb Needles over in the Wind River Range. Take a break and enjoy the view. When we were here the clouds raced across the sky, obscuring the sun enough to reveal the subtle beauty of the Absaroka Range. On days like this, these mountains are quite photogenic.

You begin the knee-buckling 2,000-foot descent to the East Fork by dropping steeply to a post directly beneath you, about two-tenths of a mile. Get out your compass, as well as your binoculars, and glass due east. You'll see a post 0.3 mile away. On your way there, look for the next post directly beneath you (southeast). You'll have to invent your own switchbacks to circumnavigate a dry tributary of Tepee Creek. Follow the posts. They will take you to the headwaters of Tepee Creek, a welcome sight. At 22.7 miles, the trail turns left and crosses Tepee Creek on a footbridge. At 23.5 miles, arrive at a meadow where the trail disappears just beyond a post. Look for a blaze on a big fir to the left of the post about 75 yards away. Skirt the meadow to the left and find another blaze on a small lodgepole pine. Just beyond this, the trail reappears. This meadow is the site of an extremely overused outfitter camp.

At about 24 miles, the trail runs out a ridge above the steep lava gorge of Tepee Creek, then heads steeply down via switchbacks, eventually heading down a rocky segment that conjures up memories of Bright Angel Trail in the Grand Canyon. Cross Tepee Creek at 24.7 miles. A huge Douglas-fir is down across the creek at this point; climbing over it is the easiest option. The last 0.25 mile of Tepee Creek Trail goes through a beautiful forest of giant Douglas-fir before ending at East Fork Trail. Turn right and walk the 2 miles of East Fork Trail back to the trailhead.

22 Eagle Creek

Highlights: A walk up a long and scenic wilderness valley with a rare glimpse of old-growth forest, uncommon in the Greater Yellowstone ecosystem.

Type of hike: Out-and-back backpack.

Total distance: 20 miles.

Difficulty: Moderate.

Maps: USGS Eagle Creek, Pinnacle Mountain, and Eagle Peak quads; Shoshone National Forest map, North Half.

Finding the trailhead: From Cody, Wyoming, follow U.S. Highway 14/16/20 for 43 miles west to Eagle Creek Campground on the left. The hike begins at the fisherman's parking lot. You can squeeze a vehicle in here, but leave a note on your window. The campground host panicked when we left a vehicle there for 11 days. The trail begins on the other side of a footbridge across the North Fork of the Shoshone River here.

Parking and trailhead facilities: Eagle Creek Campground (fee) has 20 units, outhouses, and bear-resistant refuse containers.

Key points:
- 0.2   Eagle Creek Trail junction.
- 1.0   Washakie Wilderness boundary.
- 7.0   Cabin Creek.
- 10.0   Eagle Creek Meadows.

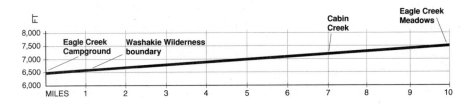

The hike: From the footbridge over the North Fork of the Shoshone River, follow the trail through a Forest Service summer-home area. At 0.2 mile, turn right onto the wide and well-maintained Eagle Creek Trail and enter the deep, lush, and exotically beautiful primeval forest of Eagle Creek. This is quite a contrast to what is normally encountered in the Yellowstone ecosystem. You encounter many big trees from here to Eagle Creek Meadows.

At 1 mile, you reach the Washakie Wilderness boundary. Past the boundary, the canyon tightens. The trail traverses a narrow contour well above Eagle Creek, providing good views of the canyon, as well as some of the basins in the high country. At 1.2 miles, enter an old-growth forest of Douglas-fir. Although not the huge specimens found along the Suiattle River of Washington's Glacier Peak Wilderness or in the haunting, but threatened,

Eagle Creek • Paradise Valley
Fire Memorial Trail • Sheep Mesa

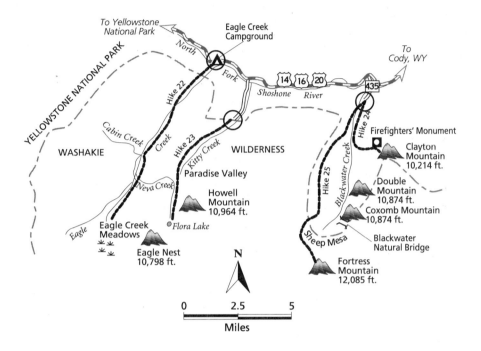

roadless areas surrounding the Kalamiopsis in Oregon, they nonetheless are unique in Greater Yellowstone. At 1.6 miles, the canyon widens, and at 2 miles, you come to a stand of magnificent old growth cottonwood. You then come top a swift and deep ford of Eagle Creek at 2.9 miles. The trail that continues along the right (east) bank of Eagle Creek will end in 30 feet, 50 feet before a gravel bar that provides an easy ford. Pick your way through the vegetation and ford at the gravel bar. The trail is just across the creek. There are six more fords within the next 0.5 mile. Wear sandals throughout this entire section. At 3.5 miles, two more fords can be avoided by following an obvious side trail for 100 yards. At 3.7 miles, leave the narrow gorge behind and emerge into a wide and glorious canyon. Majestic, conifer-cloaked walls tower 2,000 vertical feet above you. Now enter an area where we found the trail flagged in August 1996. A new trail will likely have been cut by the time you get here. At 3.9 miles, ford Eagle Creek again. Now you stay on the right (west) side of Eagle Creek for 5.1 miles.

At 5.1 miles, the trail enters a large swath of avalanche devastation. At 5.2 miles, for the first time, climbing begins in earnest and the trail switchbacks steeply. At 5.5 miles, you reach a fine view down Eagle Creek

View north across Eagle Creek Meadows. RALPH MAUGHAN PHOTO

Canyon. Now you really climb for the next 0.5 mile. The switchbacks are as steep as they can be and still be called "switchbacks." The high country around Eagle Peak towers beyond in the distance. At 6.8 miles, the trail begins its descent to Cabin Creek, which you ford at 7 miles. From here the trail climbs steadily as it circumnavigates a deep canyon of Eagle Creek. At 7.5 miles, it tops out on a long set of magnificent cliffs with good views of the canyon far below, and Eagle Peak and Pinnacle Mountain as well. Just beyond, cross an old fence line. Follow along the cliffs and enjoy superlative views for more than a mile, then descend to ford Eagle Creek where there is a Forest Service sign that says "9 miles." The creek is cold, high, and swift. Once you are on the other side, the trail enters an old-growth Douglas-fir forest, with the biggest trees in Eagle Creek. At the end of the stand, on the right, pass the queen of them all and bow before her magnificence.

At 9.5 miles, arrive at a stream that flows swiftly, but has a log for crossing. Finally, at 10 miles, you reach massive Eagle Creek Meadows. The scene is framed by high mountains, cliffs, and abundant grassland and marsh. Don't expect to be alone, however, because many horse packers camp here. The meadows contain acres of wetlands that provide excellent habitat for moose, sandhill cranes, kestrels, and many others.

23 Paradise Valley

See Map on Page 113

Highlights: Beautiful meadows, mountain scenery and Flora Lake.
Type of hike: Out-and-back day hike or backpack.
Total distance: 15 miles.
Difficulty: Moderate.
Maps: USGS Chimney Rock, Eagle Creek, and Pinnacle Mountain quads; Shoshone National Forest map, North Half.

Finding the trailhead: Drive 40 miles west on U.S. Highway 14/16/20 from Cody, Wyoming, to Forest Service 448 on your left (south). This road immediately crosses a bridge over the North Fork of the Shoshone River and arrives at the junction with FS 446. Follow gravel FS 448 and go straight up Kitty Creek. It leads past a summer home area as it climbs 600 feet to the undeveloped trailhead at 2 miles. You can park in the shade at this trailhead, elevation 7,200 feet.

Parking and trailhead facilities: Undeveloped.

Key Points
- 1.8 Paradise Valley.
- 5.5 Neva Creek Valley.
- 7.5 Flora Lake.

The hike: This trail is suitable for a day hike, although the trip to Flora Lake is best done as an overnighter. Kitty Creek and Neva Creek flow through gentle, flower-filled meadows, unlike the unseen rugged drainages on both sides of this subalpine paradise. These meadows are best in August when full of wildflowers, but not so full of mosquitoes as they are earlier.

There are several informal trails at the trailhead. After parking, continue up the road. In about 150 yards, a wide trail (another old road) leaves to the left. Do not stay on the old logging road, which is the road to your right at this junction. Now on the wide trail, you soon reach the boundary sign for the Washakie Wilderness. Here the trail narrows and climbs steeply up the forested canyon of Kitty Creek. As you climb, enjoy the nice views through the forest of the rugged Absaroka Range north of the highway in the seldom-traveled North Absaroka Wilderness. Kitty Creek runs below and generally away from the trail through a gorge in this section of the hike. In

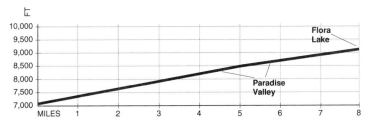

Horse party in Neva Creek. RALPH MAUGHAN PHOTO

August, you can usually find a crop of several kinds of berries in the lower canyon of Kitty Creek and also in its rugged, trail-less tributaries that flow across the trail. Be alert for bears.

After 1.7 miles, the trail gradually levels out at about 8,700 feet, and the trail-side slowly becomes meadow rather than forest. You suddenly emerge into Paradise Valley, a gently sloping, linear valley filled with wildflowers, a tranquil stream, and old-growth forest on either side of meadows that extend for about one and two-tenths miles. Moose and elk are common and the area is good bear habitat. As you look at the moose-cropped short willows near Kitty Creek, you just know you are about to see a bear. Water is plentiful in Paradise Valley, including several springs. The low ridge on the west side of the valley provides dramatic views into Eagle Creek after a short cross-country hike. Higher, but not especially rugged, mountains form the east side of the valley.

The trail continues up through Paradise Valley to an almost imperceptible divide (reached at 4.5 miles) between it and the Neva Creek drainage. Shortly after crossing this divide (elevation 9,375 feet), you come to a gap in the valley's east ridge through which Neva Creek drops steeply to join Eagle Creek far below. Many people stop at the gap to admire the distant views of Eagle Creek and Crouch Creek and the rugged mountains, including the highest mountain in Yellowstone, Eagle Peak. Follow the trail 5.5 miles past the gap and into Neva Creek's gentle valley, almost a copy of Paradise Valley except the elevation is slightly higher. The valley of Neva Creek, too, is full of flowers and water. The mountains on its sides are higher and more rugged than in Kitty Creek. Howell Mountain (elevation 10,964 feet) rises to the east, and the lower slopes of impressive Eagle Nest rise to the west. The trail ends at small, shallow, but appropriately named, Flora Lake (elevation 9,800 feet) at 7.5 miles.

Options: If you continue just past Flora Lake, the landscape changes completely. From the upper lip of Neva Creek Valley, your view falls into a rugged tributary of seldom-traveled Eyrie Creek. From this tremendous drop-off are powerful views of the black rock pinnacles, buttresses, and mesas of the wildest part of the Absaroka crest just southeast of Yellowstone. These mountains harbor permanent snowfields and small glaciers. Although you have to scramble up the slope on the west a bit to see it, the views of Sheep Mesa to the east are particularly impressive.

24 Fire Memorial Trail

See Map on Page 113

Highlights:	An enjoyable day hike through a 55-year-old forest fire scar; a moving memorial to firefighters who lost their lives at their work.
Type of hike:	Out-and-back day hike.
Total distance:	8 miles.
Difficulty:	Moderate.
Maps:	USGS Clayton Mountain and Chimney Rock quad. Shoshone National Forest map, North Half.

Finding the trailhead: Driving west from Cody on scenic U.S. Highway 14/16/20, travel 24.3 miles through remarkable Shoshone Canyon to the Shoshone National Forest boundary. Add 12.7 miles to this westward trip and you come to the first firefighters' memorial and a large sign marking the Blackwater Creek Ranch. Leave the highway here and travel south across the river atop an older steel bridge, across another wooden bridge spanning Blackwater Creek, through a pole gate, and up to a large sign south of some corrals marking the trailhead. Actually, this trail is open to vehicles for another 2 miles beyond this sign, but this is four-wheel-drive stuff, and even jeepsters are going to be unhappy if they meet a vehicle coming from the opposite direction on this narrow path. At the road's/trail's end, beside the waters of Blackwater Creek, is a sweet little camping spot.

Key points:
   0.0   Blackwater Creek ford.
   4.0   Main memorial.

The hike: Between August 20 and August 24, 1937, an intense fire consumed much more than the 1,254 acres of forest it blackened. A sudden gale-force wind on August 21 whipped the fire into a roaring inferno. Fifteen men died and 39 more were injured as the blaze raced up the mountainside on which they were working. A stone and brass memorial now stands high on the northern slopes of 10,219-foot Clayton Mountain to honor those men.

From the trailhead, your first dozen steps wade Blackwater Creek. Then it's a gentle journey through an intricate forest that contains every conifer imaginable, including juniper and Colorado blue spruce. Just over 1 mile later the trail forks. Someone has shredded most of the signs on this trail, but journeying left or southeast and across the Blackwater Creek's east fork (a rock hop at this point) sends you moderately upward for a couple of miles to the fire's point of origin.

After hiking so many areas in this sector of Wyoming that were crisped by the 1988 fires, it's refreshing to touch a forest where the new-growth trees are 30-plus feet high, demonstrating first-hand that the land does heal itself. For 2 miles the trail switchbacks up a steeper hill and to a ridgetop. The views of high peaks to the south and of the valley below spreading northwest toward Yellowstone become more magnificent with every step of elevation gain.

At 4 miles beyond that first crossing of Blackwater Creek, you will come upon the main memorial. It's a beautiful work of rock art that overlooks the entire valley. From here you can easily trace the broad path of the fire, see the rocky gully in which the men tried to escape its heat, and read their names on the brass marker.

Clayton Mountain from the West Fork of Blackwater Creek. RALPH MAUGHAN PHOTO

A trail does continue beyond the memorial and to the top of Clayton Mountain. Due to budget cutbacks and bear activity (this is prime grizzly habitat), the Forest Service has ceased maintaining this part of the trail. You may have to cross some washouts attempting this climb. The trail has a few steep grades, but it's remarkably rockless and easy to walk. Bring some water, as the gullies of Clayton Mountain are a bit stingy in that regard.

25 Sheep Mesa

See Map on Page 113

Highlights:	A 4,400-foot climb with options for exploration in beautiful, wild country. The lower part of Blackwater Creek can serve as an easy day hike, leading to a view of Blackwater Natural Bridge.
Type of hike:	Out-and-back day hike or backpack.
Total distance:	20 miles.
Difficulty:	Difficult.
Maps:	USGS Chimney Rock, Sheep Mesa, and Clayton Mountain quads; Shoshone National Forest map, North Half.

Finding the trailhead: From Cody, Wyoming, drive west on U.S. Highway14/16/20 for 37 miles to well-marked Forest Service 435 on your left (south). Drive over a steel bridge that crosses the North Fork of the Shoshone River and bear right. Go through the Blackwater Creek Ranch, which includes some corrals and gates. The road turns south, becomes rough, and makes a tough, but brief, climb up a side hill into Blackwater Creek. The road does not really require a four-wheel-drive vehicle, but it helps. High clearance is absolutely necessary. At 1 mile, you come to an informal parking area at a small wide spot where the first tributary canyon appears.

Parking and trailhead facilities: Undeveloped.

Key points:
- 1.5 Junction with West Fork Trail.
- 5.3 Subalpine meadows.
- 10.0 Fortress Mountain (elevation 12,085 feet).

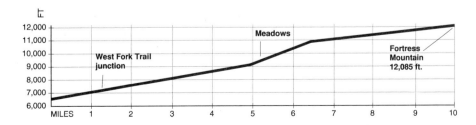

On top of Sheep Mesa looking to the northwest over Sheep Creek. RALPH MAUGHAN PHOTO

The hike: If you are venturing all the way to Sheep Mesa, you must be prepared for very bad weather, including hail and snow, at any time of the year. You can reach the lip of the cirque basin at the head of the West Fork in one long day's backpack. The lower canyon requires no special precautions except a can of pepper spray, because grizzlies can be found at any place in Blackwater Creek any time during the summer or autumn.

The trail immediately fords Blackwater Creek and crosses to its right side. The ford is not difficult, except in June. You stay on the creek's right (west) side almost all the way to Sheep Mesa. The goal for a day hike is the small meadow at the forks of Blackwater Creek. The trail, busy and well-worn with horse parties, travels up a canyon where a surprising variety of trees struggle through the harsh volcanic rock of the Absaroka Range.

It is 1.5 miles to the forks and the point where the Fire Memorial Trail heads towards Clayton Mountain. Here you gain a good, but distant, view of gigantic Blackwater Natural Bridge near the canyon rim up the main fork of Blackwater Creek. On a bright, cloudy day, the bridge can be easily mistaken for a rectangular patch of snow near the skyline. You get an even better view if you climb a short distance up the sagebrush slope to your right. (Note: The natural bridge itself is not accessible up the main fork except by a tough bushwhack.)

Most of the horse parties turn around at the meadow or ford Blackwater Creek and head up the main fork toward the memorial. You, however, do not ford the stream. Your hike continues up the West Fork Blackwater Creek with very little change at first except for much less trail traffic. The trail keeps to the right of the stream, which you do not have to cross the creek for. The path is forested, increasingly with monotonous lodgepole pine. You stay about 80 feet above the creek, but can descend in many places for water. The descent is more than a brief stroll, however.

You get only occasional views of the surrounding mountains, which are growing increasingly rugged on the creek's east side. The climb is fairly steady, but not steep, for about 2 miles. At an elevation of about 8,900 feet, the canyon becomes moister, and a few springs emerge from the ground. At 9,200 feet and 4.5 miles, the trail begins a steep climb of about 500 vertical feet up the eroded cirque wall of the upper West Fork. You soon cross the creek, an easy ford. Near the top of the climb, at 5.2 miles, you begin to enter subalpine meadows. Views appear of the rugged mountains to the north and of the tremendous walls of Sheep Mesa around you. At about 9,700 feet, an unmapped natural bridge appears above you to your left (east). While not as large as Blackwater Natural Bridge, it is, nonetheless, impressive. You are now in bighorn sheep country. I observed about ten of them right under the bridge.

The walk into the big cirque at the head of the West Fork is straightforward. It is a beautiful, tundra-filled basin with steep, mostly cliffed cirque walls all around it. The easiest way to attain the mesa's top is to climb up the slope to your right (west), to the divide between the West Fork and rugged, awesome Sheep Creek. This is the long way to the view of the natural bridge, however. A more direct route is a somewhat risky scramble through the narrow cliff bands to the southeast. Once on top, walk around the mesa until you are heading northeast. You can see down into the cirque basin at the top of the main fork of Blackwater Creek. It contains several permanent snowfields. Continue northward on this broad mesa top until you can see the gigantic natural bridge across Blackwater Creek to the east. Even if weather drives you back before you reach the natural bridge, the views are worth the trip.

This mesa top may look easy on the map, but the top of Sheep Mesa is exposed to high winds, and is a gathering place for summer thunderstorms. Given a perfectly clear dawn, thunderclouds often form and by midmorning, bringing vicious lightning and hail large enough to be injurious. Many summers the area around the top of Sheep Mesa is home to a large number of grizzly bears. Numerous overturned boulders are evidence of their foraging.

For the adventurous, you can follow Sheep Mesa southward all the way to its high point at Fortress Mountain at 12,085 feet.

26 Hardpan Lake

Highlights:	Spectacular views; wildlife viewing access to Wapiti Ridge, one of the largest and most striking escarpments in the Yellowstone ecosystem.
Type of hike:	Out-and-back backpack.
Total distance:	22 miles.
Difficulty:	Strenuous.
Maps:	USGS Flag Peak, Wapiti, Twin Creek, and Ptarmigan Mountain quads; Shoshone National Forest map, North Half.

Finding the trailhead: From Cody, Wyoming, drive 21 miles west on U.S. Highway 14/16/20 to Green Creek Road, which is on your left immediately before the Red Barn Store. Follow this paved road 1.5 miles to a fork. Bear left on a dirt road (unsigned Forest Road 406) and start climbing. Pass a cattle guard and Shoshone National Forest sign 0.2 mile later. Two miles from the Red Barn Store the road degrades into a very rough dirt road. Low-clearance vehicles need to proceed with caution as big rocks can rip out an oil pan or tear off an exhaust system. At 2.3 miles, arrive at a ford of Green Creek that is difficult in high water. Low-clearance vehicles usually scrape bottom. After the ford, climb 100 feet to a bench and small campsite on your right. Low-clearance vehicles park here. The last 0.7 mile is for high-clearance, four-wheel-drive vehicles only. If you make it to the end of the road, you'll find ample parking and a sign that reads "Table Mountain Trail No. 715, Hardpan Creek 5, South Fork 10." The trail heads up Green Creek on its right (west) side.

Parking and trailhead facilities: Undeveloped.

Key points:
- 3.7 Green Mountain (elevation 9,709 feet).
- 5.5 Bridge over tributary of Hardpan Creek.
- 10.5 Headwaters of Hardpan Creek.
- 11.0 Hardpan Lake.

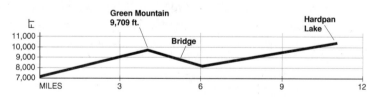

The hike: The trail ascends through lodgepole pine, Douglas-fir, and aspen and forks within 0.5 mile. Look for a very damaged signpost behind thick deadfall. You need to be alert because in the summer of 1997, a very large Douglas-fir was down across the left fork, making it difficult to see. The trail to Hardpan Creek continues just beyond the signpost. The trail to the

Hardpan Lake

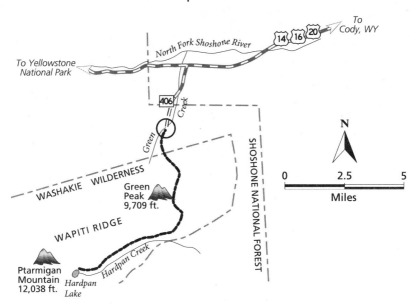

right disappears on a steep and remote finger of Wapiti Ridge. The left fork crosses Green Creek 100 yards later and begins a very steep ascent of Table Mountain. The trail is wide and easy to follow as it climbs continuously. At 2 miles, the trees thin out and the canopy becomes mostly whitebark pine and subalpine fir. You get spectacular views of the peaks of the North Absaroka Wilderness, as well as the mighty ramparts of Wapiti Ridge. In July the wildflower display is truly extraordinary. At 3 miles, cross a gate and continue climbing. The views get better and better. At 3.2 miles, you reach a huge meadow on top of Table Mountain with an absolutely astounding view that includes all of the North Absaroka, Cody, Buffalo Bill Reservoir, Boulder Ridge above the South Fork of the Shoshone River, much of the Bighorn Basin, and on a clear day, the Bighorn Mountains far to the east.

Now you drop down into a clump of subalpine fir and pass a sign that says "Green Creek 2." Another 0.5 mile brings you to a stream and another sign that says "Hardpan Creek 3, Green Creek 2." You climb relentlessly, finally reaching Green Mountain—which is called Green 9709 on your Flag Peak quadrangle—at 3.7 miles. The view is spectacular, and includes tiny Hardpan Lake, a shimmering jewel of cold water tucked into the snowy ramparts of magnificent Wapiti Ridge. To the southeast, the South Fork is a snaking blue ribbon in a remarkable valley almost 4,000 feet below.

Now the trail takes a hard right and jogs out a side ridge before turning right at a fork at 4 miles. Watch for this junction. Then, you begin a knee-buckling 1.5-mile descent to Hardpan Creek. The footing is poor because loose rocks. At 5.5 miles, cross a bridge over a narrow tributary of Hardpan Creek and pass through a rather large and unsightly outfitter camp. The trail heads upstream into the narrow canyon of Hardpan Creek, the roar of which is so loud that conversation becomes difficult when the creek is high. It crosses many side streams on its way to Hardpan Lake, some of which have blown out in the floods of 1996 and 1997.

At 7 miles, you arrive at a deep and spectacular volcanic gorge. The trail climbs steeply above it before arriving at a V intersection at 7.5 miles. Bear right. The trail continues to climb until it is very high indeed above Hardpan Creek. The forest is now whitebark pine, Engelmann spruce, and Douglas-fir. The trail emerges from the trees for a fine view of the giant cirque of Hardpan Lake.

Now you descend steeply before fording a major tributary of Hardpan Creek at 9.2 miles (a difficult ford in high water). At 9.7 miles, the trail disappears in a meadow at an outfitter camp. You pick it up again as it crosses a dry streambed on the other side of the meadow. At 10.5 miles, cross now-tiny Hardpan Creek and emerge from the trees into the country directly beneath the cirque of Hardpan Lake. The waterfalls at the outlet plunge into a beautiful and small volcanic gorge before undulating out into the flower-chocked (in mid-July) alpine meadows that you stand in. Hike another 0.5 mile to Hardpan Lake on switchbacks. The waterfalls of the outlet stream thunder downstream to your immediate left as you climb. Wapiti Ridge (*Wapiti* means elk in Shoshone) wraps around Hardpan Lake, and the surroundings are alpine in character.

Options: You can climb Wapiti Ridge on the outfitter trail that leaves from the right side of Hardpan Lake. The view from the top of Ptarmigan Mountain is incredible.

On the way to Hardpan Creek. LEE MERCER PHOTO

27 Houlihan Creek

Highlights: Spectacular views; wildlife.
Type of hike: Out-and-back day hike.
Total distance: 9 miles.
Difficulty: Strenuous.
Maps: USGS Ptarmigan Mountain and Twin Creek quads; Shoshone National Forest map, North Half.

Finding the trailhead: Take Wyoming 291 (South Fork Road) south from Cody. At 27 miles, turn right (west) on Park County 6EH, descend into a valley, and cross over the bridge the South Fork at 29.5 miles. Turn left at a T intersection and drive 0.3 mile downstream. You come to BLM land and the Bobcat-Houlihan Trailhead at 29.8 miles.

Parking and trailhead facilities: Undeveloped; however, plenty of room for parking at an improved parking lot in the bottom of the valley.

Key points:
0.3 Shoshone National Forest boundary.
0.5 Bobcat Trail junction.
1.5 Houlihan Creek.
4.5 Ridgetop.

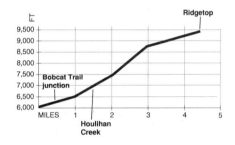

The hike: From the parking lot, follow an old (closed) dirt road west toward the mountains. The road soon becomes a trail. At 0.3 mile, you reach a fence and a gate—the Shoshone National Forest boundary. At 0.5 mile, you come to the Bobcat Trail junction. Bobcat Creek is to the south and Houlihan Creek is to the north (the right fork of the trail). Keep right and continue through open country a short distance into the mouth of Houlihan Creek, which you reach at 1 mile. The trail goes up into the broad mouth of this soon-to-become impassable gorge. The trail side is big sagebrush with cottonwood trees and wildflowers in June. Houlihan Creek itself flows down a wash with steep sides, evidence of the flash floods that roar down from its bare rock headwaters. Wood ticks were present in this area even in early July. If the weather is not hot and you had a late start, this place has very pretty afternoon views toward Carter Mountain to the east.

The trail continues up into Houlihan Creek a brief distance, but then climbs very steeply to the left up a clay side hill into the first tributary canyon to Houlihan, which you reach at 1.5 miles. Soon the steep part ends and you continue up the now generally forested side canyon (unnamed). Much of summer a small stream beneath the trail serves as your water source. Interspersing the gradual climb are a number of short, steep pitches, then the trail leaves the streamside to eventually top out on a gentle ridgetop

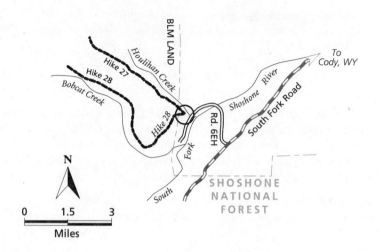

at 3 miles. No water is available once you leave the creek. The open ridge rises all the way to the base of Citadel Mountain (elevation 11,896 feet). The trail is cairned and easy to follow at first, staying near the top of the ridge. The views are spectacular in all directions. To your right (northeast), you look down into the highly dissected, rugged, impassable headwaters of Houlihan Creek.

The trail grows steeper and becomes fainter as you continue to follow the ridge. It gradually turns into a game trail and fades out among large pinnacles at an elevation of 9,400 feet and a distance of 4.5 miles. The ridge area is exposed to lightning, but it is easy to drop off its south side if weather requires. This is a nice mid-June hike, except for the ticks, mosquitoes, and grizzly bears. You may see deer and antelope in the lower area.

Options: From 9,400 feet (near the base of Citadel Mountain's 2,500-foot-tall cliff band), head south off-trail for 1.5 tough miles toward where the Bobcat Trail (Hike 28) meets elevation 8,210 on your Ptarmigan Mountain quad. From here return to the trailhead on the Bobcat Trail, a rigorous 10.5-mile loop.

Across the valley of the South Fork Shoshone River to Carter Mountain from the Houlihan Creek Trail. RALPH MAUGHAN PHOTO

28 Bobcat Creek

See Map on Page 126

Highlights: A pleasant hike up a pretty canyon.
Type of hike: Out-and-back day hike.
Total distance: 10 miles.
Difficulty: Moderate.
Maps: USGS Ptarmigan Mountain and Twin Creek quads; Shoshone National Forest map, North Half.

Finding the trailhead: See the Houlihan Creek hike (Hike 27).

Parking and trailhead facilities: See the Houlihan Creek hike (Hike 27).

Key points:
1.5   Bobcat Creek.
5.0   Point 8,210 Ptarmigan Mountain quad.

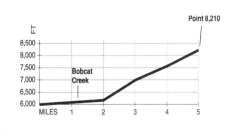

The hike: From the parking lot, follow an old (closed) dirt road west toward the mountains. The road soon becomes a trail. At 0.3 mile, you reach a fence and a

gate—the Shoshone National Forest boundary. At 0.5 mile, you come to the Bobcat Trail junction. The Bobcat Trail is an easy walk at the base of foothills for the first 1.5 miles. This section through open rangeland is very pretty in June with its high-desert wildflowers and views of the South Fork Shoshone Valley, including massive Carter Mountain, which is to the east. Just before you come to the canyon, you enter Bobcat Creek's broad riparian zone with large cottonwoods, brush, sagebrush, small meadows, and continuing grand views of Carter Mountain. Bobcat is a much bigger stream than Houlihan, and it makes plenty of noise during snowmelt in May, June, and early July. Grizzly bears frequent this streamside zone early in the season; yell loudly so they can hear you over the roar of the stream.

Once you are about half a mile up Bobcat Creek, you suddenly climb 300 feet up the north side of the canyon. This takes you out of the riparian zone, into dry forest about 150 feet above the narrowing canyon. Just past a large tributary of Bobcat Creek that enters from the west, the trail descends to streamside. You soon come to a stream crossing, which is difficult until midsummer because the current is swift and the rocks are slippery. Moreover, you quickly cross back again. The second crossing is a scary jump. To avoid all this, don't descend. Remain on the side hill just north of Bobcat Creek, and then descend steeply just as you come to a tributary of Bobcat Creek flowing in from the north. Past Bobcat's tributary, you gain a steep 400 feet on a very rocky trail (round rocks, hard to walk on). Soon, however, you level out and enter coniferous forest. The views of Wapiti Ridge ahead

Looking toward the South Fork of the Shoshone from the flank of Citadel Mountain.
RALPH MAUGHAN PHOTO

diminish. The trail is easy to follow and not so rocky. It climbs gradually and soon follows the lip of the modest gorge through which tumbles the headwaters of Bobcat Creek. Past point 8210 on your Ptarmigan Mountain quad, the trail fades.

Options: A well-seasoned hiker can scramble up onto Wapiti Ridge, or at 8210 head cross-country to the northeast and then east to connect with the Houlihan Trail and make a loop (overnighter). The cross-country segment would not be difficult were it not for four headwater tributaries of Bobcat Creek that must be crossed. The flow of each is trivial, but the four brooks are in steep little gulches about 20 feet deep. It takes time to descend each gulch.

29 South Fork Shoshone River

Highlights:	A beautiful hike up a magnificent wilderness river.
Type of hike:	Out-and-back backpack.
Total distance:	54 miles.
Difficulty:	Moderate.
Maps:	USGS Valley, Needle Mountain, Fall Creek, Hardluck Mountain, Younts Peak, and Shoshone Pass quads; Shoshone National Forest map, North Half.

Finding the trailhead: From Cody, Wyoming, follow Wyoming 291 (South Fork Road), circumnavigating Buffalo Bill Reservoir. At 35 miles, arrive at the signed junction with Hunter Creek Road on the left. Turn left, cross the South Fork Shoshone River on a bridge, and drive 5 more miles to the signed Boulder Basin Trailhead on your left.

Parking and and trailhead facilities: Undeveloped; some room to park.

Key points:
- 0.2 South Fork Work Center—Shoshone National Forest.
- 0.5 Junction with South Fork Trail.
- 4.2 Aspen Creek.
- 7.5 Ford of Needle Creek.
- 8.5 Ford of Saddle Creek.
- 14.5 Ford of East Fork Creek.
- 14.8 Ford of South Fork Shoshone River.
- 17.0 Ford of Younts Creek.
- 19.0 Ford of Marston Creek. Marston Pass Trail junction.
- 20.5 Ford of South Fork Shoshone River. Bliss Creek Meadows.
- 22.0 Ford of South Fork Shoshone River.
- 24.5 Ford of Crescent Creek.
- 27.0 Shoshone Pass.

South Fork Shoshone River

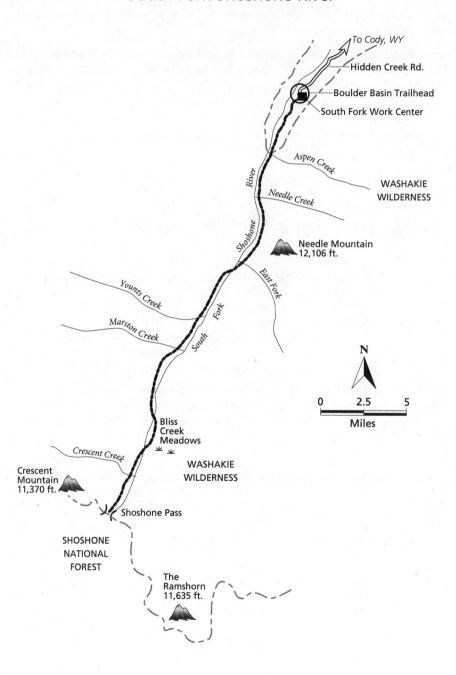

To Cody, WY

Hidden Creek Rd.

Boulder Basin Trailhead

South Fork Work Center

Aspen Creek

Needle Creek

WASHAKIE WILDERNESS

River

Shoshone

Needle Mountain
12,106 ft.

Younts Creek

East Fork

South Fork

Marston Creek

N

0   2.5   5
Miles

Bliss
Creek
Meadows

WASHAKIE
WILDERNESS

Crescent Creek

Crescent
Mountain
11,370 ft.

Shoshone Pass

SHOSHONE
NATIONAL
FOREST

The
Ramshorn
11,635 ft.

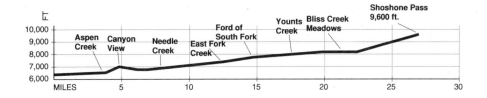

The hike: This is a long and delightful hike up a marvelous and extremely scenic wilderness valley. Glistening Absaroka peaks, deep, impenetrable lava gorges, and lush riparian meadows delight the eye. Fine camping opportunities and a well-maintained trail make this an excellent choice for the Washakie Wilderness beginner. You can walk as far as you want and return whenever you desire. You make eight fords, including only three of the South Fork, which is not bad considering the distance of the trail.

From the trailhead, turn left and continue up the road. At 0.2 mile, pass the South Fork Work Center. These folks are responsible for the fine condition of most of this area's trails. At 0.5 mile, you arrive at the signed junction with the South Fork Trail. Ascend steeply through pasture to avoid private land, and at 1.5 miles, arrive at a gate (remember to close it). You are now in a field that is crawling with longhorn steers. Within another 0.5 mile, you arrive at another gate. Close this gate as well and begin a long descent to the river. At 2.7 miles, the trail reaches the river's edge. Man and his cows are left behind; a vast and hidden wilderness valley lies ahead. At

In the South Fork Shoshone River Canyon. LEE MERCER PHOTO

4.2 miles, you reach the aptly named Aspen Creek. Ascend steeply on switchbacks until you are well above the South Fork, which is now plunging through a tight and spectacular lava gorge. The trail jogs out on a narrow ledge for about 1 mile before arriving at an astonishing view at 5.5 miles. The entirety of the South Fork, including Shoshone Pass, is visible. The huge battlements of Needle Mountain tower above you and in the distance is Shoshone Plateau. Across the canyon is a series of waterfalls, three in all, that cascade 1,000 vertical feet to the floor of the canyon.

You continue on the narrow and rugged trail, with fine views of the lava gorge below. At 6.5 miles, you start a long descent to Needle Creek, which you reach at 7.5 miles. Ford two swift, deep channels, and continue on a flat stretch of trail surrounded by lodgepole pine. At 8.5 miles, you arrive at a ford of Saddle Creek, also deep and swift. Now the canyon tightens again into another spectacular lava gorge. This long, tedious section is narrow, rugged, and steep, but the reward is fine views down into the bowels of the chasm. Eventually the trail descends to a ford of East Fork Creek at 14.5 miles, soon followed by your first ford of the South Fork at 14.8 miles. Now you follow a bench above the river in a forest that is mixed lodgepole pine, aspen, pinyon, and juniper. This is a really pleasant stretch of trail. At 20.5 miles (and after fording Younts and Marston Creeks), you reach another ford of the South Fork and enter lovely Bliss Creek Meadows. A fine swimming hole is near the ford and big canyon walls tower above. Bliss Creek

View to the east from near Shoshone Pass on the southern boundary of the Washakie Wilderness.
RALPH MAUGHAN PHOTO

Meadows are huge and continue well beyond where the trail fords the river again at 22 miles. You traverse more lovely meadows, which are becoming increasingly alpine. At 24.5 miles, you reach a ford of Crescent Creek. The mouth of this canyon is spectacular. Steep walls tower above it and in the distance, the snowy Continental Divide rises in a nearly vertical sweep.

Now you climb steeply, the trail quickly rising several hundred feet above the now much smaller South Fork. The scenery is fantastic, and the trail sees little traffic. Finally, at 27 miles, you reach beautiful Shoshone Pass, with its flower-filled meadows, alpine tarns, and good views.

30 Rampart Pass–Ishawooa Pass

Highlights:	A long, strenuous backpacking adventure; deep wilderness; spectacular scenery; wildlife viewing.
Type of hike:	Shuttle backpack.
Total distance:	67 miles.
Difficulty:	Difficult.
Maps:	USGS Clayton Mountain, Lake Creek, Sheep Mesa, Open Creek, Thorofare Buttes, Clouds Home Peak, and Valley quads; Shoshone National Forest map, North Half, Bridger-Teton National Forest map, Buffalo and Jackson Ranger Districts.

Finding the trailhead: Drive 30 miles west of Cody, Wyoming, on U.S. Highway 14/16/20 to the Elk Fork Campground on the left (south). Drive through the campground to the parking area just before the corrals. The trail begins at the signboard 100 yards beyond the parking area.

To reach the finishing point at Ishawooa Trailhead, drive southwest of Cody on Wyoming 291 (South Fork Road). Follow this 32 miles to Ishawooa Trailhead on your right. Don't confuse this with Ishawooa Mesa Trailhead, located 2.5 miles farther down the road.

Parking and trailhead facilities: Elk Fork Campground (fee) has 13 units, picnic tables, outhouses, bear-proof refuse containers and food boxes, potable water, and room for many cars. Ample parking at Ishawooa Trailhead.

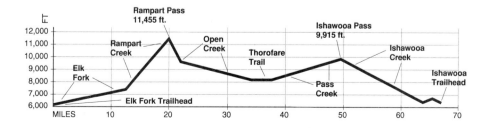

Rampart Pass–Ishawooa Pass

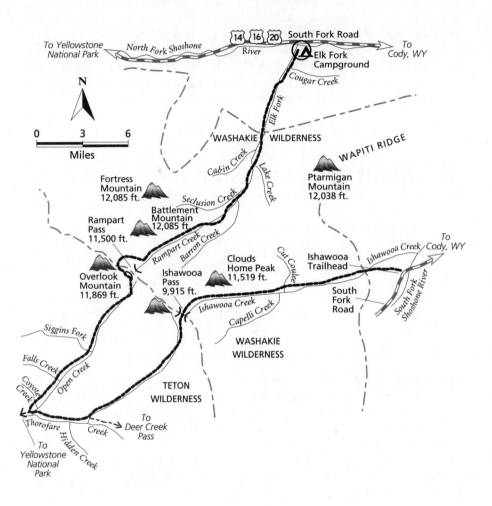

To Yellowstone National Park

North Fork Shoshone River

14 16 20 South Fork Road

To Cody, WY

Elk Fork Campground

Cougar Creek

Elk Fork

N

0 3 6
Miles

WASHAKIE WILDERNESS

WAPITI RIDGE

Cabin Creek

Lake Creek

Fortress Mountain 12,085 ft.

Seclusion Creek

Ptarmigan Mountain 12,038 ft.

Battlement Mountain 12,085 ft

Rampart Pass 11,500 ft.

Rampart Creek

Barron Creek

Clouds Home Peak 11,519 ft.

Cut Coulee

Ishawooa Creek

Ishawooa Trailhead

To Cody, WY

Overlook Mountain 11,869 ft.

Ishawooa Pass 9,915 ft.

Ishawooa Creek

South Fork Road

South Fork Shoshone River

Siggins Fork

Capelli Creek

Falls Creek

Open Creek

WASHAKIE WILDERNESS

Coyote Creek

Thorofare Creek

To Deer Creek Pass

TETON WILDERNESS

Hidden Creek

To Yellowstone National Park

Key points:

The hike: This is more than a backpacking trip—this is a pilgrimage. It proves the adage, "no pain, no gain." The reward for your toil is one of the most remarkable wilderness experiences available in the contiguous 48 states—full of spectacular scenery, wildlife viewing opportunities, and big doses of adventure. The route does not actually go over a pass, but rather directly over the 11,455-foot-high peak just south of Overlook Mountain. It gets there along a knife-edge ridge with Fishhawk Glacier 600 feet below on one side and Rampart Creek Glacier on the other. What is called Rampart Pass on the Thorofare Buttes quad looks impassable. But for simplicity's sake, we will refer to this peak as Rampart Pass. This trip is for the wilderness savvy only. The fords of Elk Fork are treacherous in high water. We also cannot emphasize enough how difficult it is to carry a heavy, multiday pack from Elk Fork Campground to the top of Rampart Pass. Allow a rest day before climbing Rampart Pass. The Open Creek side of Rampart Pass is highly eroded and not passable by horses. We recommend that hikers use two walking sticks (a pair of retractable trekking poles is best) for the descent, which is the most difficult described in this guidebook.

Despite all that, this is the deluxe way to see the Thorofare country on foot. Upper Open Creek is the only place in the Thorofare to escape horse traffic. The scale of the landscape and its scenic grandeur is unsurpassed. Few venture up Rampart Creek. Fewer still make it all the way to Rampart Pass. Could you be one of them? If you hesitate before answering yes, our advice is to choose another hike.

From the trailhead, the Elk Fork Trail ascends the massive and beautiful valley of the Elk Fork of the Shoshone River. The bizarre and sublime summits of the North Absaroka Wilderness tower behind you. Ahead and in the far distance are the three canyons that constitute the headwater streams of the Elk Fork: Seclusion, Rampart, and Barron Creeks. The middle canyon, Rampart Creek, is your destination, some 13-plus miles away. As you walk up Elk Fork, many impressive views of Wapiti Ridge (the largest and mightiest escarpment in the Yellowstone ecosystem) are revealed. You will almost certainly meet horse parties along the river as outfitters from Cody bring their guests in and out of the Elk Fork all summer long.

At 2.5 miles, pass Cougar Creek Trail and shortly thereafter, cross Cougar Creek. Then, at 3 miles, arrive at the first ford of Elk Fork, a treacherous ford before August 1. The way the trail fords is deep and swift and we don't recommend crossing here. Instead, go upstream about 100 yards to the mouth of a volcanic canyon of Elk Fork. You find a gravel bar of sorts here, but the current is still very swift and you must exercise extreme caution. Arrive at the next ford at 4.2 miles. The trail then fords back 0.5 mile later. These fords are impossible in high water. Instead, follow a faint path upstream, eventually coming to a cliff wall on the river. Pick your way around the cliff in shallow water and pick up a faint trail that crosses an unnamed stream (it drains 10,219-foot-high Clayton Mountain) and takes you to the top of a bluff well above the Elk Fork. This is big country, all only 4.5 miles from the busy East Entrance Road. From here you descend back to the trail and continue upstream on the west side of the river.

At 6 miles, arrive at the fourth ford of Elk Fork, due east of point 7001 on your Clayton Mountain quad. The location of the ford on the map is incorrect. It fords right at the mouth of that tiny stream shown on your quad (perhaps because of the gravel bar there.) Within 0.5 mile, you ford back. Walk upstream about 150 feet until you see the shallows. For the next 2 miles, the trail goes up and down along the bluffs of the river, with fine views of Wapiti Ridge and the volcanic formations along the river. At 9.2 miles, arrive at the crossing of Cabin Creek. You arrive at a relatively easy ford at 9.5 miles. Now the trail disappears as it crosses a huge meadow with excellent views of Clouds Home Peak and to the west, Blackwater Natural Bridge. Head south-southwest across the giant meadow and find the main trail on the east side of the Elk Fork. A more distinct side trail leads across the river to an active outfitter camp that is busy all summer long. Stay on the increasingly faint main trail that heads upriver toward the gates of Rampart Creek.

At 11 miles, cross Lake Creek. The trail now disappears amid much flood debris. Walk upstream and enter the "braided area" shown on your Lake Creek quad. At 11.5 miles, ford Elk Fork near some big cottonwoods, and at 12.2 miles, arrive at a cliff wall and another ford. Ford back 200 yards later. The trail is nonexistent here due to the scale of the flooding. The easiest way is to walk in sandals along the river and ford frequently, when cliffs or other obstacles thwart further progress. At 12.7 miles, pass the narrow mouth of aptly named Seclusion Creek.

Finally, at 13.2 miles, arrive at the mouth of Rampart Creek. The faint trail to Rampart Pass begins on the east side amid much flood debris and landslide activity, an indicator of things to come. The going is very tough here as you step over deadfall and scramble over landslides. At 13.6 miles, ford Rampart Creek. Now the faint trail heads up the side of the canyon, avoiding the next two fords shown on your quad. It looks as if the trail has been washed out, anyway. You struggle along a contour above the raging creek on a barely discernible track. This is really tough going and very tiring with a heavy pack. Interestingly enough, in season this section is rich in wild raspberries, rare in the Yellowstone ecosystem. We recommend you fill your belly when you take a break. Keep in mind that horses can't negotiate Rampart Creek because of the significant damage to the trail. This is a big plus for those who seek solitude. You'll find it up Rampart Creek.

Finally, at 14.2 miles, you ford Rampart Creek again and begin a steep ascent around a giant, steep, and narrow canyon that contains several spectacular waterfalls. The trail is good here and easily followed. At 14.7 miles, you reach the falls. You cannot see them from the trail, however, and a difficult descent to a bench is required to get a view. Be careful because there is some danger of a fall. At 15.2 miles, you arrive at another ford that is swift, but shallow. Over the next 5 miles the trail gradually climbs toward Glacier Basin. Your progress is interrupted frequently by huge avalanche scars, which have created walls of deadfall. They are tedious to negotiate, to say the least. At 20.2 miles, you arrive at the headwaters of Rampart Creek, where the trail disappears at an outfitter camp. Take a deep breath and revel in the remoteness of your location. The wall you see to the southwest is the Rampart Pass on your Thorofare Buttes quad. In the same direction is a large meadow with superb views of Rampart Creek Glacier and the towering cliff walls that close in upon Rampart Creek. Elk, moose, and bighorn sheep are frequently sighted here, as are grizzly bears. The multitude of bones that festoon this entire area is eerie beyond description. It's easy to see how predators can corner their prey in this glacial-carved volcanic landscape with no easy avenues of escape.

From the outfitter camp, turn sharply right (northwest) and find the trail again in the trees at the meadow's edge. It is very faint, but possible to follow. The trail climbs very steeply toward the pass on switchbacks (visible from the meadow). It is a 2,200-foot climb in 2 miles on a marginal trail, although the route is well cairned. Our advice is to start early, as a thunderstorm up on the ridge would be dangerous. You must take adequate water (at least 2 quarts) up with you because the next available water is a long 3.5 miles away at the headwaters of Open Creek. A pile of old wire and blasting caps used in the construction of this trail litters the ridge near the top of this epic ascent. Perhaps these artifacts of wilderness history will still be here when you pass this way. We trust they will. At the top, stop for the stunning view of Overlook Mountain, Fishhawk Glacier, Wapiti Ridge, Thorofare Buttes, Pinnacle Mountain, and the Trident. An old signpost marks the Teton Wilderness boundary and the junction with Open Creek Trail.

The descent is on a faint, heavily eroded footway that switchbacks very steeply over volcanic rocks, dropping 2,000 feet in 1.5 miles. Allow a minimum of two hours for this amazingly steep descent. Having hikers' trekking poles or two sturdy walking sticks is a must here. Stay focused and alert, and take it a step at a time. We stared at the top of a bull elk's head for well over an hour as we descended. We got very close to him before he realized something was amiss. He acted as if he had never encountered people before. Finally you reach a grassy bench and leave the volcanic rocks behind. But there is no time to rejoice, because your toil is not yet done. Follow the cairns across the bench to a stand of stunted subalpine fir. The trail proceeds to the edge of a cliff above a spectacular waterfalls. Faint switchbacks appear to your left and take you down to Open Creek, which you reach at

Basin below Rampart Pass. LEE MERCER PHOTO

23.7 miles. The three headwater streams of Open Creek tumble over 11 waterfalls before reaching the valley floor. This high mountain basin is like a great amphitheater, so sounds are amplified dramatically. Open Creek is the largest tributary of Thorofare Creek. Rugged mountains line the sides of the canyon most of its distance. Except for its upper portions, it has an excellent trail. Open Creek is very beautiful and remote, and it offers a world-class wilderness experience.

Open Creek Trail proceeds downstream on a faint track with some dead-fall, but nothing too difficult. After 1 mile, you arrive at a ford of Open Creek and enter a large and beautiful meadow. The trail is well maintained from here to the Thorofare. It alternates between forest and meadow, before arriving at an outfitter camp at 28 miles. From here, the trail leaves the meadows behind and enters a lodgepole-pine forest. At 32 miles, you arrive at the ford of Siggins Fork. Beyond this, the trail sees much horse use and becomes much wider. At 34 miles, cross Falls Creek, and at 34.7 miles, cross through a large and unsightly outfitter camp in a meadow. Cross Coyote Creek at 35.5 miles and then reach the signed junction with the Thorofare Trail at 36.0 miles. This trail is a horse highway through the wilderness.

You turn left, descend 100 feet to Open Creek, and ford. At 37.5 miles, pass the unsigned junction with Hidden Creek Trail to your right in a narrow part of the canyon. It is obscure and easily missed. At 39 miles, arrive at the even more obscure junction with Pass Creek Trail to your left, at a large outfitter camp in a meadow, prior to the crossing of Pass Creek. Walk through the outfitter camp, heading upstream along Pass Creek. The trail appears amidst the deadfall from the Mink Creek fire. At 0.2 mile from the junction, it disappears in an area of especially bad deadfall, at a meadow's edge. It reappears as a very obscure path on the opposite side of the meadow. For the next 2 miles, the going is tough because of heavy deadfall, but the route is obvious. At 41.2 miles, the trail disappears again at a meadow where towering Ishawooa Cone appears in the distance for the first time. Continue across the meadow, which is quite wet in spots, before arriving at more deadfall, where the trail reappears. For the next 1.5 miles, the trail is relegated to obscurity amidst the worst deadfall yet encountered. Finally, at 42.7 miles, the trail emerges from the burned forest along Pass Creek to the verdant subalpine meadows that dominate its upper reaches. From here on, the trail is distinct, even though the burn continues to cling tenaciously to the landscape.

For the next 5 miles, the trail meanders across series after series of these meadows, with Pass Creek running peacefully through the middle. Thorofare Buttes and Ishawooa Cone tower above this peaceful scene, reflecting the late-day sun in magnificent tapestries of color. At 48 miles, you arrive at a crossing of Pass Creek, now a tiny mountain stream. From here the trail begins a 1-mile, 500-foot climb to Ishawooa Pass. Except for Ishawooa Cone, directly above you amid a jumble of broken volcanic rocks, the view at the pass is unspectacular.

From here the trail is called the Ishawooa Trail, and it switchbacks through green forest to the headwaters of Ishawooa Creek, at 50.7 miles. The trail continues its gradual descent through cool, shady forest for the next 1.5 miles, but don't let that fool you. The Ishawooa Trail is a hot, dry, and rugged footway with few camping opportunities for 10 miles. However, the deeply-incised volcanic canyons, strangely eroded volcanic pinnacles, and spectacular Absaroka Range scenery help keep the mind off the trials of the trip. For most of the way, Ishawooa Creek roars several hundred feet beneath you, and all you can do is continue walking on a narrow trail cut in the wall of the gorge. At 56.5 miles, you arrive at the signed junction with the trail up Lapelli Creek. No information is available about this trail, although the spectacular scenery up Lapelli Creek Canyon looks inviting. The huge pinnacle at the confluence of Lapelli Creek and Ishawooa Creek is stunning. Continue east and at 57 miles, cross a primitive bridge across Cut Coulee. You are high above the creek now. For the next 2 miles, the trail runs near the rim of a spectacular lava gorge of Ishawooa Creek. Buttes, pinnacles, and needles contrast with waterfalls, small patches of dense lodgepole pine, and snow-capped peaks. At 59 miles, the trail begins a steep, rugged, and somewhat slippery 2-mile descent on switchbacks to Ishawooa Creek. Be careful. Most falls occur at the end of a long day when hikers are most fatigued. At 63 miles, arrive at the former site of a pack bridge and the ford of Ishawooa Creek. At 64 miles, the trail begins to climb into the Ishawooa hills, land of sagebrush and rattlesnakes (in stark contrast to what you've seen along the rest of this hike). The trail climbs steeply for 2 miles through the hills to a gate at the top, where you get a fine view of the South Fork Shoshone River, Boulder Ridge, and Wapiti Ridge. From here, it is 1 mile downhill to your car and the trailhead.

Options: Although the mouth of Hidden Creek is only a narrow slot easily overlooked by passersby, it is probably the most spectacular canyon in the Teton Wilderness. Once you get past its obscure entrance, the tremendous scenery increases all the way to its head, 3 miles from the Thorofare Trail, where an icy cold waterfall plunges off the Thorofare Plateau.

First find the trail to Hidden Creek halfway between Open Creek and Pass Creek on the Thorofare. The easiest way to find it is to start looking for a tight canyon across Thorofare Creek about 30 minutes after fording Open Creek. There are two obscure trail junctions, both unsigned. Then you have to ford Thorofare Creek, usually impossible until August 1. After this, the trail is obvious and climbs steeply for 1 mile before reaching a series of beautiful meadows with spectacular views of Thorofare Plateau. At 3 miles, the trail ends at an outfitter camp. From here, smaller trails radiate out in all directions, inviting exploration. You'll need a copy of the USGS Thorofare Plateau quad for this option.

31 Deer Creek–Ishawooa Pass

Highlights:	A popular hike to the Thorofare; nice views.
Type of hike:	Shuttle backpack.
Total distance:	50 miles.
Difficulty:	Strenuous.
Maps:	USGS Valley, Clouds Home Peak, Thorofare Buttes, and Open Creek quads; Bridger-Teton National Forest map, Buffalo and Jackson Ranger Districts, Shoshone National Forest map, North Half.

Finding the trailhead: From Cody, Wyoming, drive southwest on Wyoming 291 (South Fork Road), circumnavigating Buffalo Bill Reservoir. Follow this 40 miles past a bumper crop of housing developments to the primitive Deer Creek campground on your right. The finishing point, Ishawooa Trailhead, is on your right 8 miles before Deer Creek Campground.

Parking and trailhead facilities: Ample parking, seven campsites, and outhouses are available.

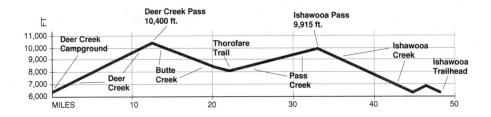

Key points:

The hike: The Deer Creek Trail is the only trail in the Washakie Wilderness used primarily to get to the Teton Wilderness. At 21 miles, it is by far the fastest way to go, which makes it extremely popular with horse parties. It is the route of choice for outfitters headed to the Thorofare, and dozens of parties can pass you in a day. Further complicating things is the fact that Deer Creek's lower portion is a tremendous gorge. The trail keeps high on the canyon wall. A beautiful and exciting hike can quickly become a tense series of moments between horse packer and hiker. It is possible a rider could be thrown from a horse in places on this trail and fall 500 feet into the chasm. No camping is available for the first 11 miles due to topography, so make sure to start early.

The Deer Creek Trail starts with a very steep climb of 900 feet on switchbacks up the dry, hot face of Ishawooa Mesa. Here, you have fine views of Carter Mountain across the South Fork Shoshone River. At 1 mile, the trail enters the gorge. Deer Creek churns unseen down in the bowels of the earth, in an awesome chasm to your left. At 2 miles, you reach the trail's first reliable drinking water. Here the trail crosses a rock-bottomed tributary that leaps over several waterfalls into the gorge. Past the tributary, the trail climbs even higher above Deer Creek, then gradually drops down to the creek where the chasm ends near a ford, which you reach at 3.5 miles.

The middle reaches of the canyon afford you some good views of the Absaroka Range and the high mountains that form the canyon's walls, rising in astonishing abruptness 3,000 feet from the banks of Deer Creek. Early enough in season, waterfalls tumble down tributary streams and rugged mountain beauty surrounds you. The trail climbs steeply over rough terrain, so this can be a tiring stretch, especially if it is hot. At 6 miles, arrive at the forks of Deer Creek. Gobblers Knob, at more than 10,000 feet, appears to sit in the middle of the canyon here. At 7.5 miles, you reach the next crossing of Deer Creek and enter another chasm, this one much shorter than the lower one.

Finally, at 10 miles, reach the top of Deer Creek Pass after the last of those steep, rocky switchbacks. The pass is between two gray-walled mountains. The one to the south is Kingfisher Peak. The one you pass directly under is lower and unnamed. Some of the seven spectacular and odd summits of Thorofare Buttes are visible to the immediate northwest. The view from the pass is also spectacular down both Deer Creek and Butte Creek. You can see from Thorofare Plateau to Carter Moun-

Deer Creek–Ishawooa Pass

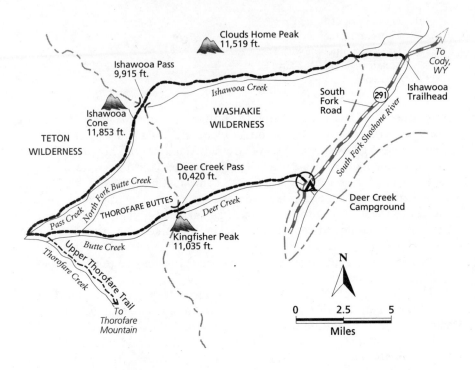

lain, a distance of nearly 40 miles. Butte Creek, in contrast to the deep V-shaped canyon of Deer Creek, is not nearly as steep or rocky. The abundance of grassy meadows is a welcome sight after the hot, tonsil-jarring ascent up Deer Creek.

Butte Creek Trail descends steeply for about 500 feet from the pass. The grade slackens at 11 miles. From here to the Thorofare Trail (another 10 miles), you follow a moderate grade downhill. At 12 miles, the trail approaches Butte Creek. It then follows a downward-sloping bench for the next 2 miles. You pass through a number of small openings with fine views of Thorofare Buttes. At 14 miles, you arrive at the first of several crossings of Butte Creek. These are rock hops by mid-July. You arrive at the North Fork of Butte Creek at 18 miles. Butte Creek is larger now. At 21 miles, you reach Thorofare Creek at its confluence with Butte Creek, near a giant outfitter camp. At 22 miles, arrive at the crossing of Pass Creek. Just beyond this, Pass Creek Trail begins at a large outfitter camp and this takes you to Ishawooa Pass. Refer to Hike 30, beginning at mile 39, for the rest of the hike description.

Options: The old outfitter trail that traverses the upper Thorofare is a spectacular side trip. This country is the farthest from a road in the contiguous 48 states. It is also the loneliest place on the Thorofare, seeing much less horse traffic.

From the outfitter camp at the confluence of Butte Creek and Thorofare Creek, ford Butte Creek and head upstream on the Thorofare. The trail appears in the tall grass about 100 yards beyond the ford and crosses many large meadows, with fine views of Yellow Mountain. At 4 miles, you ford Valley Fork and begin to circumnavigate a spectacular lava gorge before entering giant meadows that are 3 miles long. At 8 miles, the trail seemingly ends across the creek from a littered outfitter camp. Several trails continue upstream from here. The lowest is the most used, and you can follow this across a bench high above the Thorofare. Thorofare Mountain comes into view at 9 miles. The trail drops to a crossing of Thorofare Creek at 10 miles and ascends a series of steep and faint switchbacks to the basin beneath Thorofare Mountain. Permanent snowfields surround you, and the steep ramparts of Thorofare Mountain tower above, inviting exploration. You can climb the peak, using the ridge that is north-northeast of it. Although it is all talus, the footing is good until right beneath the peak, where you have to traverse an area with high exposure. There is a register on the summit.

The view is as spectacular as any described in this guide and includes the entire Teton Range, 30-plus miles away. Younts Peak, the source of the Yellowstone River, is seemingly right there for the touching. Mighty and sublime Thorofare Plateau, the most remote and unforgiving escarpment in the Yellowstone ecosystem, unfolds to the south. Directly beneath you at the bottom of a 3,000-foot-high wall is Younts Creek. In fact, you can see the Absaroka Range, Pinnacle Buttes, Wind River Range, Gros Ventre Range, and Snake Range. Few places command such a view. Here, amid the lofty

At the forks of Deer Creek. RALPH MAUGHAN PHOTO

heights of Thorofare country, the need to preserve all roadless areas is revealed. What can you do? Gandhi said not to be discouraged by how small your efforts seem. Anything you do will help.

Front Range

32 Eastern Washakie Wilderness Loop

Highlights: Four high passes; breathtaking scenery; light traffic.
Type of hike: Backpacking loop.
Total distance: 30 miles.
Difficulty: Strenuous.
Maps: USGS Francs Peak, Dunrud Peak, Wiggins Peak, Mount Burwell quads; and Shoshone National Forest map, North Half.

Finding the trailhead: Your destination is Kirwin, an abandoned mining town and trailhead. From Meeteetse, Wyoming, drive west 6.5 miles on Wyoming 290 and turn left on the signed Wood River Road, which is 0.2 mile beyond the bridge over the Wood River. Seven miles later the pavement ends and the road becomes good gravel. One mile later the road bears sharply right (west) at a T intersection and crosses the Wood River again on a small bridge, where it immediately turns left and continues upriver. At 17.5 miles from Meeteetse, cross the Shoshone National Forest boundary. A sign indicates Kirwin is 12 miles ahead. (Kirwin is an abandoned mining town that is a minor tourist attraction.) At 21 miles, pass Brown Mountain Campground on the left. Between here and Jojo Creek, the road becomes gumbo when wet and is high above the river, resulting in hazardous driving conditions. At 23 miles, arrive at Jojo Trailhead and the ford of Jojo Creek. This ford is difficult for a low-clearance vehicle when Jojo Creek is high and it would be hazardous after a heavy rain. JoJo trailhead is not a bad place to park under these circumstances. It is 6 miles to Kirwin from here, but it can be walked in 2.5 hours. If still driving, continue through the Double D Ranch and ford the Wood River at 23.2 miles. In low water this can be done in a low-clearance vehicle. At 25.2 miles, reach the second ford of the Wood River. If you have a low-clearance vehicle, this is as far as you can go. If you have a high-clearance vehicle, it is a rocky 3.5 miles to Kirwin. This section of the road was closed in the summer of 1998 for several days on two occasions by landslides. Keep this in mind. If it has been a wet summer, we recommend parking at Jojo Trailhead.

Parking and trailhead facilities: Ample parking, primitive camping, and two outhouses are available. The hike begins beyond the gate (south) at the road's end.

Key points:

- 1.6   Junction with Horse Creek Trail.
- 2.1   Junction with East Fork Trail.
- 3.3   Sign indicating route to Bear Creek Pass.
- 4.3   Bear Creek Pass.
- 5.0   Junction with Absaroka Trail.
- 7.0   Unnamed pass.
- 9.0   Caldwell Creek.
- 12.0 Junction with Wiggins Fork Trail.
- 13.5 Burwell Pass.
- 15.7 Cow Creek.
- 20.0 Junction with Greybull River Trail.
- 23.0 Steer Creek.
- 25.0 Yellow Creek.
- 26.8 Greybull Pass. Brown Basin Trail junction.

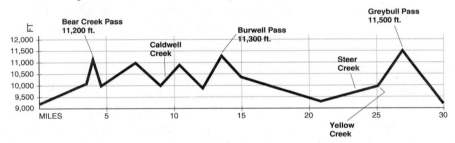

The hike: The Front Range of the Absaroka rises sharply above the plains of the Big Horn Basin and reaches its apex at 13,153-foot-high Francs Peak. The massive and spectacular Greybull River drains a large part of this country, and is plugged like a main circuit cable directly into the snowfields of the high Absaroka near the pass that bears its name. The Greybull is a sacred river for Native Americans—named for a white buffalo that once wandered this country. This hike encompasses the upper Greybull as well as some of the East Fork Wind River country and provides you with a continuously marvelous visual experience that rivals anything found in the overcrowded Wind River Range. Best of all, this area sees very little use aside from hunting.

From Kirwin, the trail gently climbs a huge alpine valley under a retreating canopy of subalpine fir and Engelmann spruce. At 1 mile, arrive at a locked cabin and the road's end. A small sign indicates you are on Trail 443, an excellent footpath, that heads southwest and rapidly climbs above the Wood River. At 1.5 miles, you cross Horse Creek and then immediately climb over an old fence before arriving at the signed junction with Horse Creek Trail at 1.6 miles. The trail to Bear Creek Pass continues up a wide alpine valley with fine views of the lofty places that surround you. At 2 miles, the trail crosses the Wood River and plunges into a dark forest of subalpine fir, Douglas-fir, and Engelmann spruce. At 2.1 miles, you arrive at the signed junction with East Fork Trail. Continue southwest, following the now much smaller Wood River upstream. For the next 0.5 mile the trail remains in the forest before crossing the river again at 2.6 miles and leaving the trees. At 2.8 miles, you cross and immediately recross the Wood River as

146

Eastern Washakie Wilderness Loop • Yellow Creek Loop
Cascade Creek Loop • Meadow Creek Basin

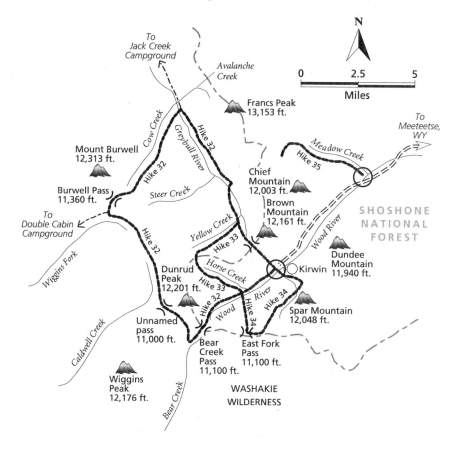

you circumnavigate a steep wall. Now you climb in earnest with spectacular views of Dunrud Peak. Get out your binoculars and glass the slopes for game. At 3.3 miles arrive at a sign that points to Bear Creek Pass. From the sign, Bear Creek Pass is a 1-mile climb. The Washakie Wilderness boundary is at the top, and the view is good. The trail switchbacks steeply toward the headwaters of Bear Creek. The trail appears and disappears frequently as it meets with many recent landslides. In spite of this, it is easy to follow, and at 5 miles, you reach the signed junction with the Absaroka Trail. Turn right (north) and ascend on an obvious trail for about 0.5 mile. From here the trail is well cairned as it climbs to an unnamed pass high in the Absaroka. This section is truly jading with a pack on. However, the scenery is grand. A massive lava gorge containing a tributary of Bear Creek plunges downward in a series of spectacular cascades to your left. The high peaks of this remote section of the Absaroka Range tower around you. Large elk herds and bighorn sheep often browse the giant meadows.

At 5.7 miles, arrive at a deep gorge running into the tributary from the west. Look right, up canyon, and spot a cairn about a quarter of a mile away. At this cairn a clear trail takes you down into the gorge and back out again. Cairns then lead you to the edge of the main gorge on your left in another 0.5 mile. A trail appears that takes you through another, smaller gorge. Again the trail disappears, but the cairns lead you back uphill. Just when you're ready to lynch the authors, a set of switchbacks appears at 6.7 miles. At 7 miles, you arrive at the unnamed pass high in the Absaroka Range. Gaze back whence you came and see a view of incredible scale that includes the Absaroka Range and much of the Wind River Range, scraping the sky to the south. The very rugged trail leads northwest and most importantly, downhill. You now travel among sublime and bizarre Absaroka volcanics. Lava spires, petrified wood, and crystal festoon this incredibly scenic area. Footprints are nonexistent, and horse traffic is minimal. For the next 0.5 mile you cross a small stream several times. Now the giant and spectacular walls of the Black Canyon are before you, an incredible scene. The walls are 1 mile away but appear close enough to touch. Continue downhill through rock slides to another stream crossing, which can be rock hopped. The trail is slightly washed out here and it ascends a steep bank that is very slippery when wet. Climb around a very steep lava gorge in heavy timber. This is an extraordinarily beautiful section. The whitebark pine and cow parsnip are drawing cards for grizzly bears, and much fresh sign was evident in July 1996. At 9 miles, arrive at the headwaters of Caldwell Creek (Black Canyon) and a sign that reads "Absaroka Trail."

From the Absaroka Trail. LEE MERCER PHOTO

Wiggins Fork Trail to Burwell Pass. LEE MERCER PHOTO

From here, the trail climbs slowly across a giant alpine meadow with spellbinding scenery. The volcanic rocks of the Absaroka Range reflect light differently at different times of day and the scale is barely comprehensible. Each step is a new exercise in wonder. After 1 mile, the trail side hills and climbs around a tight gorge before reaching a saddle at 10 miles. From here, massive Wiggins Peak and Mount Burwell tower above the landscape in an incredible alpine setting. You then start a long, gradual descent into the headwaters of Wiggins Fork. At 12 miles, arrive at the unsigned junction with Wiggins Fork Trail and the end of the Absaroka Trail. All that remains of the old sign is a weather-beaten white pine post. The trail is engulfed by a forest of Douglas-fir, subalpine fir, and Engelmann spruce and bends southwest with the Wiggins Fork Canyon, but you want to turn right sharply and head north across the small meadow, which is the beginning of the heavily switchbacked route to Burwell Pass. If you arrive at the ford of Wiggins Fork, you've gone 1 mile too far. At 13.5 miles, you arrive at the top of Burwell Pass and the sign that indicates its elevation of 11,360 feet. Take in the superlative view that includes Mount Burwell, an unnamed (climbable) peak to the southeast, Crescent Top, the Continental Divide, and Francs Peak. Large elk herds are often found on the slopes of Mount Burwell. Keep your eyes open.

The trail descends 0.5 mile on switchbacks, crosses a small stream (the headwaters of Cow Creek), and descends to a large bench near tree line at 14.5 miles. The trail is marked by posts for 0.3 mile. At tree line, bear left and the footway reappears. Now it descends steeply. There are fine views of

Francs Peak in this section. At 15.7 miles, the trail crosses Cow Creek. At 16 miles, the valley widens considerably with good views toward the Greybull River, Avalanche Creek, and Francs Peak.

At 17 miles, the trail switchbacks downhill and arrives at another ford of Cow Creek, followed by yet another crossing at 18 miles. You now traverse the area of worst flood deposition in the Cow Creek drainage. The valley widens again and you pass a small outfitter camp at 19 miles. Shortly thereafter, you cross the North Fork of Cow Creek. For the next mile the trail climbs around the spectacular narrow gorge of Cow Creek as the creek tumbles wildly toward its confluence with the Greybull River. The trail reaches a bluff above the river with spectacular views of the ramparts of Francs Peak, the steep and sublime reaches of Avalanche Creek, and the now-distant Burwell Pass.

At 20 miles, reach the ford of the Greybull River, just north of the mouth of Cow Creek. For the next mile, the Greybull River Trail has been obliterated by the massive amount of debris that poured out of the steep and rocky canyon of Avalanche Creek (obviously aptly named) during the 1997 flood. Look for cairns. Once it leaves the flood deposition of Avalanche Creek, the trail emerges onto a bench above the Greybull River with a breathtaking view of Yellow Ridge. The scale of the Upper Greybull is Alaskan. It is truly one of our country's great wilderness rivers. If you look downstream from here, you can see the country around Boulder Pass, more than 10 miles away. At 23 miles, you arrive at beautiful Steer Creek, a vast and wide valley that begs to be explored.

Over the next 2 miles the Greybull River Valley becomes an alpine valley. We saw a bald eagle in this section. About half a mile above Steer Creek, the trail emerges from tree line and starts to climb steadily. At 25 miles, you arrive at the crossing of Yellow Creek (the headwater stream of the Greybull River). Unlocked and broken-down Yellow Creek Cabin is just above the crossing. There are spectacular views up Yellow Creek and down the Greybull River from here. The trail turns east-northeast in front of the cabin and skirts a stand of subalpine fir before bending back south and climbing steeply. At 25.5 miles, you reach a high alpine basin beneath the lofty summits of the Absaroka. The trail becomes somewhat faint here. Greybull Pass is generally south, while the river bends around to the southwest. Refer to the Francs Peak quad and your compass here. At 26 miles, cross the Greybull and begin a very steep ascent on switchbacks toward the pass. The route is faint, but well marked with cairns. The footway is poor and the rock is loose, making the ascent even more tiring. Finally, at 26.8 miles, reach Greybull Pass at 11,470 feet, the highest elevation of this hike. Enjoy the fine views in all directions.

From here the steep switchbacks of Brown Basin Trail begin. You drop 2,300 feet in 3.2 miles to Kirwin. Brown Basin is a spectacular hanging valley that is generally snow-blocked until mid-July in most years. At the bottom a wooden sign denotes Brown Basin Trail. It's behind the gate due north of the register box, 100 yards from the Kirwin trailhead.

33 Yellow Creek Loop

See Map on Page 147

Highlights: Incredible scenery; a chance to see wildlife.
Type of hike: Day hike or backpacking loop.
Total distance: 12 miles.
Difficulty: Strenuous.
Maps: USGS Francs Peak and Dunrud Peak quads; Shoshone National Forest map, North Half.

Finding the trailhead: See the Eastern Washakie Wilderness Loop (Hike 32).

Parking and trailhead facilities: See the Eastern Washakie Wilderness Loop (Hike 32).

Key points:
1.5   Horse Creek ford.
1.6   Horse Creek Trail junction.
4.0   Horse Creek headwater ford.
7.0   Greybull River.
8.0   Greybull River ford.
8.8   Greybull Pass (elevation 11,470 feet).

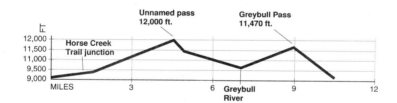

The hike: This hike gives the hiker a good overview of the rugged mountain beauty of the Absaroka Range. However, physical conditioning is essential on this difficult loop.

From Kirwin, the trail gently climbs a huge alpine valley under a retreating canopy of subalpine fir and Engelmann spruce. At 1 mile, arrive at a locked cabin and the road's end. A small sign indicates you are on Trail 443, an excellent footpath, that heads southwest and rapidly climbs above the Wood River. At 1.5 miles, you cross Horse Creek and then immediately climb over an old fence before arriving at the signed junction with Horse Creek Trail at 1.6 miles. Turn right and begin ascending on switchbacks. You climb relentlessly. At 4 miles, cross a headwaters stream of Horse Creek, with the steep walls of the Absaroka Range surrounding you. That little notch to the west-northwest is where you're headed and is as steep as it looks. The last 0.5 mile is really tough. Finally, at 4.5 miles, you reach an unnamed pass and the Washakie Wilderness boundary at 12,000 feet. The view is phenomenal.

Yellow Creek (right) and headwaters of the Greybull (left). View off-trail looking to the west.
RALPH MAUGHAN PHOTO

Now descend steeply on a faint trail to the headwaters of Yellow Creek (also the source of the Greybull River). Once you reach Yellow Creek, the trail disappears entirely. The northwest side is the easiest walking. Stay above the willows. At 7 miles, you reach the Greybull River at unlocked and broken-down Yellow Creek Cabin. The trail turns east-northeast in front of the cabin and skirts a stand of subalpine fir before bending back south and climbing steeply. At 7.5 miles, reach a high alpine basin beneath the lofty summits of the Absaroka. The trail becomes somewhat faint here. Greybull Pass is generally south, while the river bends around to the southwest. Refer to the Francs Peak quad and your compass here. At 8 miles, cross the Greybull River and begin a very steep ascent via switchbacks toward the pass. The route is faint, but well marked with cairns. The footway is poor and the rock is loose, making the ascent even more tiring. Finally, at 8.8 miles, reach Greybull Pass at 11,470 feet. Enjoy the fine views in all directions.

From here the steep switchbacks of Brown Basin Trail begin. You drop 2,300 feet in 3.2 miles to Kirwin and your rig. Brown Basin is a spectacular hanging valley that is generally snow-blocked until mid-July in most years. At the bottom a wooden sign denotes Brown Basin Trail. It's behind the gate due north of the register box, 100 yards from the Kirwin trailhead.

34 Cascade Creek Loop

See Map on Page 147

Highlights: Spectacular views; an incredible ridge traverse.
Type of hike: Day hike loop.
Total distance: 8.5 miles.
Difficulty: Strenuous.
Maps: USGS Francs Peak and Dunrud Peak quads; Shoshone National Forest map, North Half.

Finding the trailhead: See the Eastern Washakie Wilderness Loop (Hike 32).

Parking and trailhead facilities: See the Eastern Washakie Wilderness Loop (Hike 32).

Key points:

1.5 Horse Creek ford.
1.6 Horse Creek Trail junction.
2.0 Wood River ford.
2.1 East Fork Trail junction.
3.6 East Fork Pass.
5.0 Cascade Creek Trail.
6.0 Smuggler Gulch Trail junction.
6.5 Cascade Creek ford.
8.2 Wood River ford.
8.3 End of Cascade Creek Trail at Wood River Trail.

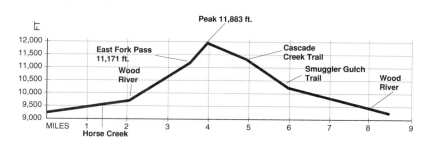

The hike: This is a tough hike, but the scenic rewards more than justify the effort. It includes some exhilarating off-trail hiking at high altitude across a narrow ridge. This hike is not for the beginner. Conditioning is key, and basic route-finding skills are essential.

From Kirwin, the trail gently climbs a huge alpine valley under a retreating canopy of subalpine fir and Engelmann spruce. At 1 mile, arrive at a locked cabin and the road's end. A small sign indicates that you are on Trail 443, an excellent footpath that heads southwest and rapidly climbs above the Wood River. At 1.5 miles, cross Horse Creek and then immediately climb over an old fence before arriving at the signed junction with Horse Creek Trail at 1.6 miles. The trail continues up a wide alpine valley with fine views of the lofty places that surround you. At 2 miles, the trail crosses the Wood River and plunges into a dark forest of subalpine fir, Douglas-fir, and Engelmann spruce. At 2.1 miles, arrive at the signed junction with East Fork Trail. Turn left onto East Fork Trail and begin the steep, arduous climb to East Fork Pass—a climb of 1,500 feet in just 1.5 miles. At 2.6 miles, you emerge from tree line and the climb stiffens. The last 0.5 mile to East Fork Pass is brutal, and a snow cornice near the top sometimes persists well into July. You reach the top at 3.6 miles.

From here, you begin what is simply the most astonishing ridge traverse described in this guide. The views include mysterious and isolated Washakie Needles, Twin Peaks, most of the Absaroka Range, and much of the Wind River Range. Head east-southeast toward the big peak closest to you. This is peak 11,883 on the Dunrud Peak quad. From here, you head east-northeast to peak 11,674. The ridge is narrow and steep, but walkable. The vertical relief on either side is not for the fainthearted. After peak 11,674, the ridge widens considerably. You descend 300 feet to a saddle and the Cascade Creek Trail at 5 miles. Turn left and descend into the rocky basin of Cascade Creek. At 6 miles, you pass the signed junction with unmaintained Smuggler Gulch Trail. At 6.5 miles, you cross Cascade Creek, and shortly thereafter the trail joins an old road that was part of the mining operation at Kirwin. The trail makes a sharp left at 7.3 miles, descends through a steep meadow,

View from East Fork Pass. LEE MERCER PHOTO

and crosses Cascade Creek again. From here, you descend steeply to a ford of the Wood River, which you reach at 8.2 miles. At 8.3 miles, the Cascade Creek Trail ends at the Wood River Trail. You turn right and return to Kirwin in 0.2 mile.

On East Fork Pass. LEE MERCER PHOTO

35 Meadow Creek Basin

See Map on Page 147

Highlights: A short, steep climb to a beautiful alpine basin.
Type of hike: Out-and-back day hike or base camp.
Total distance: 6 miles.
Difficulty: Moderate.
Maps: USGS Francs Peak and Dick Creek Lakes quads; Shoshone National Forest map, North Half.

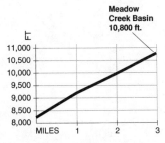

Finding the trailhead: Refer to the directions for the Eastern Washakie Wilderness Loop (Hike 32). The Meadow Creek Trailhead is just off the four-wheel-drive road about half a mile upstream from the second ford of the Wood River. The trailhead is well past the obvious mouth of Meadow Creek and is identified by a large, rusted, iron sign that says "Meadow Creek Trail." Note: In July 1998 the road and the trailhead were destroyed in a series of flash floods from monsoonal rains. As of the writing of this book, the trailhead was not obvious. Meadow Creek is the next big canyon after Jojo Creek, (2 miles upstream of it). Just head into Meadow Creek Canyon until you pick up the trail.

Parking and trailhead facilities: Undeveloped.

Key points:
- 1.5   Top of switchbacks.
- 3.0   Meadow Creek Basin.

The hike: The trail leads directly to the base of the east flank of Chief Mountain and ascends 600 feet through the forest on 21 well-constructed switchbacks. Although built very well, the switchbacks were made a long time ago, and they are beginning to fall into disrepair. At the top of the switchbacks, the scene changes completely. The trail crosses a large rockslide (fortunately the trail through the slide is fairly good). From the slide, the views of the surrounding mountain scenery are fine, especially to the southeast where the view is filled with the remarkably rugged hulk of Dundee Mountain. Dundee Mountain is the very steep southeast wall of Wood River Canyon. It rises 3,000 feet in less than 1 mile. Vegetation on its cliffs, talus slides, and pinnacles are nearly absent due to its abrupt angle and unstable slopes. Once past the rockslide, the trail levels out and enters Meadow Creek Canyon then imperceptibly rotates counterclockwise until it is heading due west. The trail remains above the creek on its left side until just below

Chief Mountain 12,003 feet, on the south side of Meadow Creek Basin. RALPH MAUGHAN PHOTO

Meadow Creek Basin. It stays high enough above the creek and the descent is so rugged, that you should not count on Meadow Creek as a source of water. Carry enough water to see you to Meadow Creek Basin.

The trail now crosses several small rockslides. The scenery is good. As you advance up Meadow Creek, the wall on the right (north) side of the creek becomes increasingly rugged. Although you can't see its top, the wall is capped by unnamed peaks 12,345 and 12,106. The wall on the left is rugged and strewn with rock.

After a climb of about 1,600 feet and a distance of 3 miles, the trail reaches the bottom of Meadow Creek Basin. The new, 1991 Francs Peak quad shows the trail staying on the left all the way to the crest of the range; in fact, the trail crosses Meadow Creek here to avoid a significant area of unpleasant boulders. Cross here unless the creek is too high. The crossing is usually not a problem after mid-July in years of normal snow and snowmelt. The creek is fairly swift, just wide enough to make a jump unwise, and the rocks tend to be very slippery. If you can't cross, struggle upstream 0.25 mile until you are past the rocks and the trail crosses back and follows the leftmost of the three headwaters forks of Meadow Creek. The entire basin is beautiful, more so in its upper part. This upper part, at about 10,400 feet, is above timberline, however, and subject to lightning and hail.

Options: Perhaps the best way of making this more than a day hike or an overnighter is to make a base camp in the lower basin and explore during the day. An ascent of Francs Peak is possible as a day hike. This peak, the highest of the Absaroka, is 4 miles to the northwest and 3,000 feet above the basin. The first feature to catch your eye will probably be rugged 12,003-

foot-high Chief Mountain, which rises on the south side of the basin. The entire climb to the basin is actually just a climb of Chief Mountain's lower east flank. Despite all those cliffs, Chief Mountain is flat on top. You can roam at will throughout the basin. There is no need to follow the trail. Every view is a scenic one. To climb to the crest of the range, continue to follow the trail. Note that Meadow Creek forks at the top of the lower basin. There is a north fork, a center fork, and a left fork. The north fork runs due south into the center fork near a decrepit cabin. Follow the obvious tread and climb steeply, but briefly, up onto a ridge that separates the center fork from the left fork. This puts you on a lovely, grassy ridgetop just below the impressive cliffs on Chief Mountain. The route is obvious and the tread of the trail is usually visible as it climbs up into the headwaters cirque of the left fork. It keeps near to the creek once you are in this steep and fairly narrow cirque basin. You may hear rolling rocks. There are often quite a few bighorn sheep in the area as well as elk. Rocks are also dislodged by snowmelt in the afternoon. Be aware that these boulders sometimes roll across the trail.

At about the 10,800-foot contour is a snowfield that covers the trail most years until late July or even later. If you climb this, you should have an ice ax for an arrest, especially early in the day when the snow is still hard. With a lot of puffing you can climb past the snow to the right of the snowfield on steep, muddy tundra with small rocks. Once past, head sharply left to find the trail again. You can also proceed directly ahead across the tundra and reach the crest of the range near peak 12,064, 2.5 miles past Meadow Creek Basin.

Cairns and a generally visible trail lead you to the pass between broad point 11,930 on Galena Ridge to the east and peak 12,104 on the crest to the right (west) in another mile. Southward beyond the pass, the trail drifts toward the Absaroka crest, which it crosses at about 11,800 feet. The tread is not visible, and it is often under snow (a huge snow cornice sits most of the summer on the trail's location shown on the Francs Peak quad). The quad shows the trail switchbacking from the crest steeply down into the headwaters of the Greybull River. We saw little evidence of a trail. It looked like a dangerous descent over high-incline volcanic rocks.

On the other hand, you can walk along the crest northward from here, almost all the way to Francs Peak. Most of the route is over 12,000 feet in elevation. The crest gives a stunning view down into the Greybull River with Yellow Ridge being the most prominent feature. From the crest you can look westward up Yellow Creek (the headwaters stream of the Greybull) into country that is roadless for 50 miles. While we were there, wind poured down Yellow Creek, hitting us at a right angle at a constant velocity of about 50 miles per hour with gusts that were impossible to stand against. It was a perfectly normal, warm alpine summer day off the ridge.

The Shoshone National Forest map and the Dunrud Peak quad show a trail crossing from Meadow Creek Basin and dropping into the Greybull. Viewed from the crest, where this trail presumably plunges into the Greybull, the idea that there might be a trail fades quickly.

158

36 Pickett-Piney Loop

Highlights:	A great variety of scenery; sublime distant views; numerous antelope and elk.
Type of hike:	Backpacking loop or rigorous day hike.
Total distance:	15.5 miles.
Difficulty:	Moderate.
Maps:	USGS Aldrich Basin, North Fork Pickett Creek, and Phelps Mountain quads; Shoshone National Forest map, North Half.

Finding the trailhead: To reach the Pickett Creek Trailhead, drive on paved Wyoming 290 south from Mceteetse, Wyoming. At 10 miles, the road splits at a Y intersection. Take County Road 41X to your right. The pavement quickly ends. Keep left at another junction; don't take the road over the Greybull River. Continue toward the mountains on the good gravel road, ignoring the turnoff to Timber Creek that you reach after 4 miles. Look for pronghorn antelope. Six miles from the end of the pavement, turn right, cross the bridge across the Greybull, and drive slowly through the ranch headquarters of the famous Pitchfork Ranch. The road forks just past the headquarters. Go left and follow the now poorer road along the north side of the Greybull. The road never gets close to the river. After a few miles, the road gradually turns about 45 degrees and heads up Pickett Creek onto Carter Mountain. The road now deteriorates. The lower Pickett Creek section can be very gooey mud after heavy rain. Then the road becomes rocky and quite rough. When you reach the junction with the Carter Mountain road (four-wheel-drive trail), you can legally park on a small piece of BLM land just left (south) of the Pickett Creek Road. Continue ahead and through the gate(s). The end of the line is on Wyoming state land at the ford of the North Fork of Pickett Creek.

Parking and trailhead facilities: Undeveloped; a few places to park.

Key points:
- 4.0   Piney Creek Trail.
- 7.5   Begin ascent to Piney Pass.
- 8.5   Piney Pass.
- 11.0   Pickett Creek fork.
- 14.0   Pickett Creek canyon.

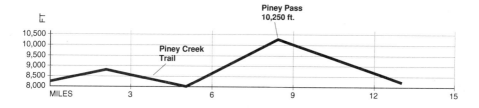

Pickett-Piney Loop

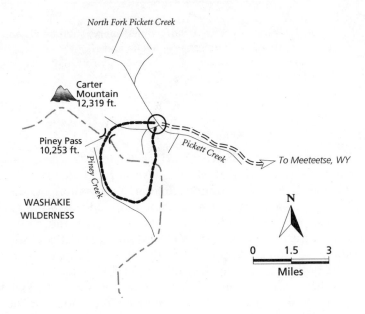

The hike: Ford the creek and follow the jeep trail to the Forest Service guard station at Pickett Creek. A bit downstream from the station find a place to ford Pickett Creek. Find a cow or elk trail and climb the embankment on the other side of the creek. Head downstream. When you have gone 0.25 mile, you will come out onto a lovely bench, especially so in mid-June to early July. Wildflowers are abundant. You get a perfect view to the east over Pitchfork Ranch and then to the ridges near Meeteetse. When the air is clear, these ridges really are purple late in the day, just as described by Western song and legend.

Walk generally south on the rolling bench land between the North Fork of Pickett Creek and Piney Creek, keeping fairly near the base of the steep mountain to your right. There are a startling number of deep marmot holes in this area. You will cross a couple of small creeks. All may be dry by late summer. As you approach the broad mouth of Piney Creek, be careful to angle downhill toward the southeast. Otherwise, you will find yourself atop rotten, dangerous cliffs. At 4 miles, reach Piney Creek Trail coming up from the famous Palette Ranch.

Once on the Piney Creek Trail, you climb gently up the canyon, which quickly narrows. The trail never crosses Piney Creek, but keeps to the north side. After the first constriction in the canyon, you gain a view of the battlements and pinnacled cliffs on Carter Mountain at the forks of Piney Creek.

At 6.2 miles, you reach the base of the spires. The scenery is stunning. As you continue, the forest, never dense, opens further into scattered fir and whitebark pine. At 7.5 miles, the steep climb to Piney Pass begins just before the trail (which continues up the left fork of Piney Creek) crosses Piney Creek. The left fork is not named on the maps, but it is as large as the main fork. Its waters trickle down from a number of 12,000-foot plus summits on Carter Mountain. You will get a grand view of some of these from Piney Pass. The trail to Piney Pass is sparsely marked with cairns, and the tread is usually not visible on the open meadowy slope. Regardless, the route is clear. Keep to the right of Piney Creek and don't drift into the shallow side drainage to your right. The route is exposed all the way to broad, treeless Piney Pass at 10,250 feet, which you reach at 8.5 miles.

The pass is a beautiful, but often windy, place. It is open country with pinnacles on the Carter Mountain ridge immediately above and to the left. To the right (southeast) is a much more gradual slope with some isolated pinnacles. Ahead and behind are fine views of Carter Mountain. Both pronghorn antelope and elk are common here. Looking north from Piney Pass, you see the treeless northern reaches of Carter Mountain and still more pinnacles. Looking to the northeast, down the unnamed south fork of Pickett Creek, you see a timbered, north-facing slope and a bare, south-facing slope. In the far distance, the steppe country on the Pitchfork Ranch is visible.

Keep to your left and descend the open tundra down an increasingly steep side canyon. As you descend, many trails appear. They are elk trails, but are also used by hikers and horse parties. It doesn't matter which path

Carter Mountain. Early July from the Piney Pass Trail. RALPH MAUGHAN PHOTO.

you take; simply drop down until you reach the fork of Pickett Creek at 11 miles. Walk downstream and pass a fence.

You can take a variety of routes down this fork of Pickett Creek. We followed elk trails, which are generally good, but disconcertingly, they often end at rock outcrops or rock slides. After about a mile of walking, an old road about 200 feet upslope to your left is another route. After about 2 miles, you reach the shallow Pickett Creek canyon. Here you meet the four-wheel-drive trail and follow it 1.5 miles downhill to the North Fork of Pickett Creek and your rig.

37 Jack Creek Loop

Highlights:	A good overnight loop that can also serve as a base camp for numerous explorations. Great views of Carter Mountain, Francs Peaks, Irish Rock, and the vast Washakie country to the west of the Greybull drainage.
Type of hike:	Backpacking loop.
Total distance:	17 miles.
Difficulty:	Moderate.
Maps:	USGS Phelps Mountain and Irish Rock quads; Shoshone National Forest map, North Half.

Finding the trailhead: Drive on Wyoming 290 south from Meetetsee, Wyoming, passing by Wyoming 200, which heads south along the Wood River. Continue on paved Wyoming 290 to a Y intersection at 10 miles. County Road 5XS forks to the left and CR 4IX to the right. Take CR 4IX and after a couple of hundred yards, keep left at another road junction (the right fork crosses a bridge over the Greybull River). In 4 more miles, pass by the road to Timber Creek Ranger Station and after 1 more mile, come to a junction. Go left for Jack Creek (the right fork heads up onto Carter Mountain and Pickett Creek [Hike 36]). After 2 more miles, pass Francs Fork road, which goes left. After 2 more miles, go left toward the south to avoid most of the Four Bear oil field. The road swings around a hill and climbs up a mountainside to some oil wells. At 24 miles from Meeteetse, in an oil field, the Phelps Mountain road exits to the left (south). You reach the Shoshone National Forest boundary in 4 more miles. The Jack Creek Campground/Trailhead is 0.5 mile beyond the forest boundary.

The large Jack Creek Trailhead is just upstream from the campground in the Jack Creek drainage, not the Greybull drainage. The Greybull "high water" trail, your return route, leaves from this trailhead (heading west) as does the Jack Creek Trail (heading south).

Parking and trailhead facilities: Undeveloped.

Jack Creek Loop

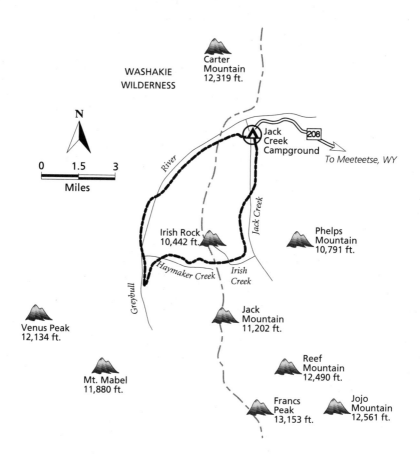

Key points:

- 2.7 Gorge and waterfalls.
- 3.0 Meadows and ponds above Jack Creek.
- 5.0 Haymaker Trail junction.
- 6.0 Crossing of Irish Creek.
- 6.5 Haymaker Pass (elevation 10,400 feet).
- 9.0 Crossing of Haymaker Creek.
- 10.0 Greybull River Trail junction.
- 13.0 High Water Trail junction.

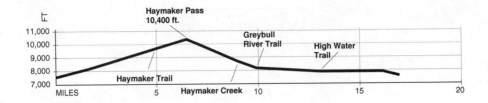

The hike: The Jack Creek Trail, a well-constructed path with a tread 1 to 2 feet wide, goes directly up the left side of Jack Creek. Use is moderate, mostly horse packers. The trail climbs steadily, but moderately, through open slopes and scattered timber. Behind you to the north are the rugged, nearly bare slopes of sprawling Carter Mountain with scattered patches of trees and badlands.

After a 600-foot climb at 1.5 miles, you come to the first crossing of Jack Creek, an easy ford in midsummer. The trail crosses from the left to the right side of the creek at the ford in a 500- to 1000-foot-deep canyon. Just past the ford, the trail climbs steeply another 600 feet on some well-constructed switchbacks and ends in a big rockslide area. The trail then drops down 100 feet to a second ford. We hopped across the rocks on July 21. The middle reach of the canyon, mostly forest with much slide topography, has a much different character than the open climb from the Jack Creek Trailhead. Past the second ford, continue upstream just briefly and cross a third time. From this point the trail has been rerouted and the location on the topo (both the old quad and the new) is wrong. The trail has been moved from the left side to the right side of the canyon. The new trail is narrow, but in good condition, and it has been elaborately constructed up the rough, cliffy, and scenic right side of the canyon. It winds, climbs, and switchbacks to the top of what has become a gorge. On top is a great view of the gorge (with a waterfall). Be very careful at the viewpoint, as the footing is crumbling breccia, full of small, loose, rounded stones.

On top, the trail traverses much different country than below. It climbs up onto and follows meadowy benches. You gain fine views of the slopes of Phelps Mountain to the east across Jack Creek. The trail eventually flattens out and meanders along a meadowy bench to a small tributary of Jack Creek at the edge of forest. Enter the forest and keep walking along the bench. At 5 miles, you reach a primitive road (used to bring livestock into upper Jack Creek). Follow the road briefly, then take the trail that leaves the road and goes to the right. This is the beginning of the Haymaker Trail. The trail climbs a bit, swings around into Irish Creek, and comes out of the forest. From here the trail climbs 1,000 feet in 1.5 miles to Haymaker Pass. Irish Rock towers just to the northwest of the trail (to the north at the pass). This high pass (elevation 10,400 feet) is the boundary of the Washakie Wilderness. There are fine views in all directions with a direct view of Francs Peak to the south, and the Greybull drainage and country behind it to the west.

From the pass, the trail drops at a moderate rate of 1,700 feet in 2.5 miles to a crossing of Haymaker Creek. Irish Rock towers behind you and is more impressive from Haymaker Creek than Irish Creek. Watch for antelope, elk,

164

and grizzly bears near Haymaker Pass and down into Haymaker Creek. The descent has scant water in August. As you climb up the opposite side of the small canyon that Haymaker Creek flows down, the trail splits. Take the more-used route to the right that follows a bench just above Haymaker Creek. It descends gradually, but then very steeply, to the Greybull River. Basalt cliffs form the last part of the steep finale. You reach a fine waterfall where Haymaker Creek leaps over the cliffs just before the trail reaches the Greybull River. At 10 miles, you reach the signed junction with the Greybull River Trail. Turn right (north-northeast).

Hiking down the Greybull River Trail is easy except for the two fords reached at 11.5 and 12.5 miles, respectively. However, the fords are not particularly difficult by midsummer if you choose the crossing point with care (the streambed is unstable and the deep spots change yearly) and wade deliberately. In high water, it is advisable to do these fords early in the day. At 13 miles, you arrive at the signed junction with the High Water Trail. It bears right through lodgepole pine, and is narrow and a little hard to see. The wider Greybull River Trail fords the river 25 feet beyond this junction. Once you are on the High Water Trail, it is easy to follow.

Follow the High Water Trail 4 miles back to Jack Creek Trailhead and your rig, fording Jack Creek one last time right before the trailhead.

Francs Peak, 13,153 feet, the highest in the Absaroka Range. RALPH MAUGHAN PHOTO.

Threatened and Endangered

Grizzly Bears
The Teton and Washakie Wilderness Areas and the adjacent country are vital to the perpetuation of the great bear, and the evidence shows that grizzly bear numbers are growing in the Washakie Wilderness. The Teton Wilderness already has about as many grizzlies as the habitat will support. In particular, there has been movement toward, and reinhabitation of, the southeastern and eastern portions of the Washakie by grizzlies. This movement may be due to the abundance of whitebark pine there.

Whitebark pine nuts are a major food source for grizzly bears in the northern Rocky Mountains. The forest fires of 1988 destroyed much of the whitebark pine in Yellowstone as well as some in the Teton Wilderness. Recent research on grizzly foods puts these pine nuts near the very top of good grizzly food sources. The Washakie also has many of the high-elevation moth sites favored by grizzlies. Army cutworm moths feed on the alpine flowers by the billions. To escape the heat, they spend part of the day in talus slides next to the unmelted summer snow. Grizzlies often feed for hours on these moths, which are 60 percent fat.

In spite of this, the federal agencies in charge of grizzly bear recovery have refused to expand the Yellowstone grizzly recovery area to include the Front Range of the Absaroka Mountains on the eastern side of the Washakie Wilderness and also the area just to the east of the wilderness. Couple this with the constant pressure from the state politicians of Wyoming to remove the Yellowstone grizzly from the threatened species list, and you have a hotbed of political intrigue that is not in the best interests of the bear.

The grizzly bear is the ultimate symbol of wilderness in our country. It is not something to be feared, but rather revered. The Greater Yellowstone Grizzly Recovery Area needs to include the entire Washakie Wilderness and the surrounding country such as the Mount Leidy Highlands and the Gros Ventre Range. Meanwhile, the wilderness traveler can happily assume there is a grizzly in just about every drainage of the Teton and Washakie Wilderness Areas at least some time during the year.

Wolves
The reintroduction of wolves to Yellowstone National Park in 1995 has been quite successful, although there is good evidence that the population growth of wolves inside Yellowstone Park proper may have halted as the various packs have staked almost all of the park as their territories. As a result, the wolves have spread, and one or two packs use the Teton Wilderness part of the year. The wolves tend to favor the broad stream valleys of the wilderness such as Pacific Creek, Atlantic Creek, and the Thorofare.

Wolves have also established themselves in the Dunoir Special Management Unit—the wild, but only partially protected niche between the Teton and Washakie Wilderness Areas. Packs have also formed to the south in the

Mount Leidy Highlands, the Gros Ventre Range, and Jackson Hole itself. Some people hope, and others fear, that the wolf may be removed from the endangered species list by 2001 or 2002.

Unprotected Roadless Areas

One of the greatest challenges we face as Americans in the new millenium is to protect all roadless areas by including them in the National Wilderness Preservation System. With the major growth in the urban centers of the American West and the explosion of outdoor recreation in recent decades, the time to act is now. What we save in the next few years is all we are ever going to save, and even then, it will only amount to less than 4 percent of the contiguous 48 states–the machine culture having gobbled up the rest with its insatiable appetite for growth. These lands represent our last link with our past; a past that has already relegated the sound of bison stampeding across the short-grass prairie to the ash heap of history. This is all that remains of the lands Lewis and Clark wandered through on their epic journey just two centuries ago.

The National Wilderness Preservation System is the last refuge of the amazing botanical diversity Lewis and Clark encountered as they traveled along the Missouri River toward its source in present-day Montana. Elk, grizzly bears, wolf, moose, wolverines, neo-tropical migrant songbirds (70 percent reduced since 1970), and many other sensitive species require roadless areas for their survival. Native fish, such as bull trout, have declined in large part due to sediment loading from logging roads on our national forests. Three areas of special concern are contiguous to the Teton and Washakie Wilderness Areas. These are the Dunoir, Carter Mountain, and Phelps Mountain unprotected roadless areas. In the case of Carter and Phelps Mountains minor road closures would dramatically expand the scale of the landscape and provide a permanent home for grizzly bears seeking new ranges.

We need your help. Our children's heritage is shrinking. They must be assured of having the same opportunities for peace, contemplation, and communion with nature that we have enjoyed. The authors of this guide have been kind enough to share a place they love with you; in return, all we ask is that you add your voice to the debate. You won't be sorry. When you stand on a high plateau deep in the Teton and Washakie Wilderness Areas, watching an elk herd two hundred strong ascend an 11,000 foot plateau in search of grasses revealed by retreating snows, you will know you have done something to preserve this ancient migration. By offering an informed opinion, you will have contributed to a force greater than the machine culture you seek to escape in the National Wilderness Preservation System.

Sierra Club Grizzly Bear Ecosystems Project
234 East Mendenhall, Suite A
Bozeman, MT 59715
406-582-8365
wildgriz@aol.com

Alliance for the Wild Rockies
P.O. Box 8731
Missoula, MT 59807
406-721-5420
www.wildrockies.org/awr
awr@wildrockies.org

Greater Yellowstone Coalition
P.O. Box 1874
Bozeman, MT 59771
406-586-1593
gyc@greateryellowstone.org

Wyoming Outdoor Council
262 Lincoln Street
Lander, WY 82520
307-332-7031

Appendix A: For More Information

The Teton Wilderness is in the Bridger-Teton National Forest. Bear-resistant food containers are available from the Forest Service. Contact the Bridger-Teton National Forest at the following addresses and phone numbers:

Bridger-Teton National Forest
P.O. Box 1888
Jackson, WY 83001
307-733-2752
btnfiunfo/r4_b-t@fs.fed.us
(Bear-resistant food containers available)

Buffalo Ranger District
Highway 287
P.O. Box 278
Moran, WY 83013
307-543-2386

The Washakie Wilderness is in the Shoshone National Forest. Contact them at the following addresses and phone numbers:

Shoshone National Forest
808 Meadow Lane
Cody, WY 82414
307-527-6241
Information_Visitor/r2_shoshone@fs.fed.us

North Zone Ranger District
203A Yellowstone Avenue
P.O. Box 1840
Cody, WY 82414
307-527-6921

Wind River Ranger District
209 East Ramshorn
P.O. Box 186
Dubois, WY 82513
307-455-2466
(Bear-resistant food containers available)

Emergency Medical Services - In case of emergency, dial 911, just like in the big city. You can find comprehensive medical services at West Park Hospital in Cody, Wyoming, and at St. John's Hospital in Jackson, Wyoming.

Appendix B: Further Reading

Biography of a Grizzly by Ernest Thompson Seton
Grizzly Years by Doug Peacock
The Grizzly Bear by Thomas MacNamee
Track of the Grizzly by Frank Craighead
Rocky Mountain Wildflowers by Frank Craighead
For Everything There is a Season by Frank C. Craighead
Rising from the Plains by John McPhee
Creation of the Teton Landscape by David Love and John Reed
The Wolf by L. David Mech
Rocky Mountain Elk by Olaus Murie
Animal Tracks by Olaus Murie
Wapiti Wilderness by Margaret Murie and Olaus Murie
Western Forests by John Kirchner and Gordon Morrison
Yellowstone: A Visitors Companion by George Wuerthner
Yellowstone and the Fires of Change by George Wuerthner
Where the Bluebird Sings to the Lemonade Springs by Wallace Stegner
A Natural History of Western Trees by Donald Peattie
A Woman Tenderfoot by Grace Gallatin Seton-Thompson
Solo on Her Own Adventure edited by Susan Rodgers
Life in Hand by Hannah Hinchman
A Trail Through Leaves by Hannah Hinchman
Off the Beaten Path: Stories of Place edited by Joseph Barbato and Lisa Horak
The Pack Goat by John Mionczynski
Journal of a Trapper by Osborne Russell
Mountain Man by Vardis Fisher
The Adventures of Captain Bonneville by Washington Irving
Amphibians and Reptiles in Yellowstone and Grand Teton National Parks by Edward Koch and Charles Peterson
John Colter: His Years in the Rockies by Burton Harris
Small Mammals of the Yellowstone Ecosystem by Donald Streubel
Birds of the Northern Rockies by Tom Ulrich
Mammals of the Northern Rockies by Tom Ulrich
Wyoming Handbook by Don Pitcher
Close Range: Wyoming Stories by Annie Proulx.
Wilderness Survival by Suzanne Swedo.
Bear Aware by Bill Schneider.
Backpacking Tips by Bill and Russ Schneider.
Wilderness First Aid by Gilbert Preston.
Avalanche Aware by John Moynier.
Leave No Trace by Will Harmon.
Reading Weather by Jim Woodmencey.

Appendix C: The Hiker's Checklist

Always make and check your own checklist!

If you've ever hiked into the backcountry and discovered that you've forgotten an essential, you know that it's a good idea to make a checklist and check the items off as you pack so that you won't forget the things you want and need. Here are some ideas:

Clothing

- [ ] Dependable rain parka
- [ ] Rain pants
- [ ] Windbreaker
- [ ] Thermal underwear
- [ ] Shorts
- [ ] Long pants or sweatpants
- [ ] Wool cap or balaclava
- [ ] Hat
- [ ] Wool shirt or sweater
- [ ] Jacket or parka
- [ ] Extra socks
- [ ] Underwear
- [ ] Lightweight shirts
- [ ] T-shirts
- [ ] Bandanna(s)
- [ ] Mittens or gloves
- [ ] Belt

Footwear

- [ ] Sturdy, comfortable boots
- [ ] Lightweight camp shoes

Bedding

- [ ] Sleeping bag
- [ ] Foam pad or air mattress
- [ ] Ground sheet (plastic or nylon)
- [ ] Dependable tent

Hauling

- [ ] Backpack and/or day pack

Cooking

- [ ] 1-quart container (plastic)
- [ ] 1-gallon water container for camp use (collapsible)
- [ ] Backpack stove and extra fuel
- [ ] Funnel
- [ ] Aluminum foil
- [ ] Cooking pots
- [ ] Bowls/plates
- [ ] Utensils (spoons, forks, small spatula, knife)
- [ ] Pot scrubber
- [ ] Matches in waterproof container

Food and Drink

- [ ] Cereal
- [ ] Bread
- [ ] Crackers
- [ ] Cheese
- [ ] Trail mix
- [ ] Margarine
- [ ] Powdered soups
- [ ] Salt/pepper
- [ ] Main course meals
- [ ] Snacks
- [ ] Hot chocolate
- [ ] Tea
- [ ] Powdered milk
- [ ] Drink mixes

Photography
- [ ] Camera and film
- [ ] Filters
- [ ] Lens brush/paper

Miscellaneous
- [ ] Sunglasses
- [ ] Map and a compass
- [ ] Toilet paper
- [ ] Pocketknife
- [ ] Sunscreen
- [ ] Good insect repellent
- [ ] Lip balm
- [ ] Flashlight with good batteries and a spare bulb
- [ ] Candle(s)
- [ ] First-aid kit
- [ ] Your FalconGuide
- [ ] Survival kit
- [ ] Small garden trowel or shovel
- [ ] Water filter or purification tablets
- [ ] Plastic bags (for trash)
- [ ] Soap
- [ ] Towel
- [ ] Toothbrush
- [ ] Fishing license
- [ ] Fishing rod, reel, lures, flies, etc.
- [ ] Binoculars
- [ ] Waterproof covering for pack
- [ ] Watch
- [ ] Sewing kit

About The Authors

Lee Mercer, a writer and explorer of remote wildernesses, has more than two decades of experience in outdoor leadership. He has dedicated his entire adult life to wilderness preservation. Although a confirmed desert rat, his love of wild places includes first and foremost the Yellowstone ecosystem. He lives in Boise, Idaho.

Ralph Maughan, a professor of political science at Idaho State University and author, along with his wife Jackie Johnson Maughan, of the FalconGuide *Hiking Idaho,* draws on three decades of wilderness experience and leadership in such groups as the Sierra Club, the Greater Yellowstone Coalition, the Wolf Recovery Foundation, and the Idaho Environmental Council. He lives in Pocatello, Idaho.

The Wilderness Society

THE WILDERNESS SOCIETY'S ROOTS

When their car came to a screeching halt somewhere outside of Knoxville, Tennessee, the passengers were in hot debate over plans for a new conservation group. The men got out of the car and climbed an embankment where they sat and argued over the philosophy and definition of the new organization.

Three months later, in January 1935, the group met again in Washington, D. C. Participants in the meeting included Robert Sterling Yard, publicist for the National Park Service; Benton MacKaye, the "Father of the Appalachian Trail"; and Robert Marshall, chief of recreation and lands for the USDA Forest Service. "All we desire to save from invasion," they declared, "is that extremely minor fraction of outdoor America which yet remains free from mechanical sights and sounds and smells." For a name, they finally settled on The Wilderness Society.

Among the co-founders was Aldo Leopold, a wildlife ecologist at the University of Wisconsin. In Leopold's view, The Wilderness Society would help form the cornerstone of a movement needed to save America's vanishing wilderness. It took nearly 30 years, but President Lyndon B. Johnson finally signed The Wilderness Act of 1964 into law September 3rd, in the rose garden of the White House.

THE WILDERNESS SOCIETY TODAY

The founders called the organization The Wilderness Society, and they put out an urgent call, as we do today, for "spirited people who will fight for the freedom of the wilderness." Today, Americans enjoy some 104 million acres of protected wilderness, due in large part to the efforts of The Wilderness Society. The Wilderness Society is a nonprofit organization devoted to protecting America's wilderness and developing a nation-wide network of wild lands through public education, scientific analysis and activism. The organization's goal is to ensure that future generations will enjoy the clean air and water, wildlife, beauty and opportunity for renewal provided by pristine forests, mountains, rivers and deserts. You can help protect American wildlands by becoming a Wilderness Society Member. Here are three ways you can join: **Telephone: 1-800-THE-WILD; E-mail: member@tws.org or visit the website at www.wilderness.org; Write: The Wilderness Society, Attention: Membership, 900 17th Street Northwest, Washington, D.C. 20006.**

FALCON GUIDES ® Leading the way™

FalconGuides® are available for where-to-go hiking, mountain biking, rock climbing, walking, scenic driving, fishing, rockhounding, paddling, birding, wildlife viewing, and camping. We also have FalconGuides on essential outdoor skills and subjects and field identification. The following titles are currently available, but this list grows every year. For a free catalog with a complete list of titles, call FALCON toll-free at 1-800-582-2665.

BIRDING GUIDES

Birding Georgia
Birding Illinois
Birding Minnesota
Birding Montana
Birding Northern California
Birding Texas
Birding Utah

PADDLING GUIDES

Paddling Minnesota
Paddling Montana
Paddling Okefenokee
Paddling Oregon
Paddling Yellowstone & Grand
   Teton National Parks

WALKING

Walking Colorado Springs
Walking Denver
Walking Portland
Walking Seattle
Walking St. Louis
Walking San Francisco
Walking Virginia Beach

CAMPING GUIDES

Camping Arizona
Camping California's
   National Forests
Camping Colorado
Camping Oregon
Camping Southern California
Camping Washington
Recreation Guide to Washington
   National Forests

FIELD GUIDES

Bitterroot: Montana State Flower
Canyon Country Wildflowers
Central Rocky Mountain
   Wildflowers
Chihuahuan Desert Wildflowers
Great Lakes Berry Book
New England Berry Book
Ozark Wildflowers
Pacific Northwest Berry Book
Plants of Arizona
Rare Plants of Colorado
Rocky Mountain Berry Book
Scats & Tracks of the Pacific
   Coast States
Scats & Tracks of the Rocky Mtns.
Sierra Nevada Wildflowers
Southern Rocky Mountain
   Wildflowers
Tallgrass Prairie Wildflowers
Western Trees

ROCKHOUNDING GUIDES

Rockhounding Arizona
Rockhounding California
Rockhounding Colorado
Rockhounding Montana
Rockhounding Nevada
Rockhounding New Mexico
Rockhounding Texas
Rockhounding Utah
Rockhounding Wyoming

HOW-TO GUIDES

Avalanche Aware
Backpacking Tips
Bear Aware
Desert Hiking Tips
Hiking with Dogs
Hiking with Kids
Mountain Lion Alert
Reading Weather
Route Finding
Using GPS
Wild Country Companion
Wilderness First Aid
Wilderness Survival

MORE GUIDEBOOKS

Backcountry Horseman's
   Guide to Washington
Family Fun in Montana
Family Fun in Yellowstone
Exploring Canyonlands & Arches
   National Parks
Exploring Hawaii's Parklands
Exploring Mount Helena
Exploring Southern California
   Beaches
Hiking Hot Springs of the Pacific
   Northwest
Touring Arizona Hot Springs
Touring California & Nevada
   Hot Springs
Touring Colorado Hot Springs
Touring Montana and Wyoming
   Hot Springs
Trail Riding Western Montana
Wilderness Directory
Wild Montana
Wild Utah
Wild Virginia

■ *To order any of these books, check with your local bookseller
or call FALCON ® at **1-800-582-2665**.
Visit us on the world wide web at:
www.Falcon.com*

HIKING GUIDES

Best Hikes Along the Continental Divide
Hiking Alaska
Hiking Arizona
Hiking Arizona's Cactus Country
Hiking the Beartooths
Hiking Big Bend National Park
Hiking the Bob Marshall Country
Hiking California
Hiking California's Desert Parks
Hiking Carlsbad Caverns
    and Guadalupe Mtns. National Parks
Hiking Colorado
Hiking Colorado, Vol. II
Hiking Colorado's Summits
Hiking Colorado's Weminuche Wilderness
Hiking the Columbia River Gorge
Hiking Florida
Hiking Georgia
Hiking Glacier & Waterton Lakes National Parks
Hiking Grand Canyon National Park
Hiking Grand Staircase-Escalante/Glen Canyon
Hiking Grand Teton National Park
Hiking Great Basin National Park
Hiking Hot Springs in the Pacific Northwest
Hiking Idaho
Hiking Indiana
Hiking Maine
Hiking Maryland and Delaware
Hiking Michigan
Hiking Minnesota
Hiking Montana
Hiking Mount Rainier National Park
Hiking Mount St. Helens
Hiking Nevada
Hiking New Hampshire
Hiking New Mexico
Hiking New Mexico's Gila Wilderness

Hiking New York
Hiking North Carolina
Hiking the North Cascades
Hiking Northern Arizona
Hiking Northern California
Hiking Olympic National Park
Hiking Oregon
Hiking Oregon's Eagle Cap Wilderness
Hiking Oregon's Mount Hood/Badger Creek
Hiking Oregon's Central Cascades
Hiking Pennsylvania
Hiking Ruins Seldom Seen
Hiking Shenandoah
Hiking the Sierra Nevada
Hiking South Carolina
Hiking South Dakota's Black Hills Country
Hiking Southern New England
Hiking Tennessee
Hiking Texas
Hiking Utah
Hiking Utah's Summits
Hiking Vermont
Hiking Virginia
Hiking Washington
Hiking Wisconsin
Hiking Wyoming
Hiking Wyoming's Cloud Peak Wilderness
Hiking Wyoming's Teton
    and Washakie Wilderness
Hiking Wyoming's Wind River Range
Hiking Yellowstone National Park
Hiking Yosemite National Park
Hiking Zion & Bryce Canyon National Parks
Wild Country Companion
Wild Montana
Wild Utah
Wild Virginia